A Professional Guide to REBT

A Professional Guide to REBT provides the reader with theoretical and detailed practical information from an experienced and qualified practitioner using and researching Rational Emotive Behaviour Therapy (REBT) day to day.

Following a logical flow, each chapter covers a core tenet of REBT aligned with how REBT is practised. The book considers and briefly presents the research evidence to date, grounding this work in evidence-based practice. Each chapter provides a brief but detailed portrayal of REBT, informing readers how the REBT tenet is applied in practice and, importantly, why.

A Professional Guide to REBT offers a thorough yet distilled guide on how the fundamentals of REBT are applied and is key reading for students, scholars, and practitioners of psychology, psychotherapy, and REBT.

Martin J. Turner, PhD, is a Reader in Psychology at Manchester Metropolitan University. He is a British Psychological Society (BPS) Chartered and Health and Care Professions Council (HCPC) Registered Sport and Exercise Psychologist, an Associate Fellow of the BPS, and a Fellow of the Association for Rational Emotive Behaviour Therapy (REBT). He is most known for his work applying REBT within performance settings. He holds an Advanced Practicum Certificate in REBT from the Albert Ellis Institute, which also awarded him the Albert Ellis Award for Research in 2018 and 2020. Martin has also received an Outstanding Achievement Award for Research from the UK Association for REBT. From 1994 to 2024, Martin is the most published and most cited REBT researcher in the world. He is a frequent keynote/invited speaker at academic conferences and industry events, delivering workshops to fellow professionals and trainees and consultancy across private and public sectors. He was the first-team psychologist for Lincoln City Football Club during the club's record breaking 2025–26 season.

A Professional Guide to REBT

Martin J. Turner

Routledge
Taylor & Francis Group
NEW YORK AND LONDON

Designed cover image: Getty Images

First published 2027
by Routledge
605 Third Avenue, New York, NY 10158

and by Routledge
4 Park Square, Milton Park, Abingdon, Oxon, OX14 4RN

Routledge is an imprint of the Taylor & Francis Group, an informa business

ISBN: 978-1-032-83257-9 (hbk)
ISBN: 978-1-032-83256-2 (pbk)
ISBN: 978-1-003-50847-2 (ebk)

DOI: 10.4324/9781003508472

Typeset in Times New Roman
by Apex CoVantage, LLC

Contents

	List of Figures	*vi*
	Foreword	*vii*
	Acknowledgements	*ix*
	Praise for previous book, The Rational Practitioner	*x*
	Introduction	1
1	Rational emotive behaviour therapy	5
2	The GABCDE framework	9
3	Setting the foundations	23
4	Consequences (C): Emotional, behavioural, cognitive	34
5	Adversity or activating event (A)	45
6	Goals (G)	50
7	Beliefs (B) in rational emotive behaviour therapy	57
8	Assessing beliefs (B)	75
9	Disputation (D)	83
10	Effective new beliefs (E)	94
11	Finishing the work, and closing remarks	106
	References	*112*
	Index	*124*

Figures

1.1	The GABCDE framework of REBT	7
2.1	Diagrammatic representation of the GABCDE framework. The dotted line between GAB and C reflects pre-REBT and the move to D and E from B reflects the REBT process	10
2.2	Diagrammatic representation of *irrational* GABC	12
2.3	Diagrammatic representation of *rational* GABC	13
2.4	An example of REBT and CAT integration	16
2.5	The interdependent GABCDE framework	19
2.6	Simplified interdependent GABCDE framework	21
2.7	Specific REBT versus general REBT	22
3.1	Example GABCDE assessment sheet from the author's work with a skeet shooter	29
4.1	The articulated GABC framework incorporating Ellisian and Lazarusian concepts	40
9.1	Client belief disputation	90
9.2	Paired components rating disputation task	92
10.1	Rational/irrational frequency dials	96
10.2	High rationality and low irrationality on the rational/irrational frequency dials	96
10.3	The rational credo	99
10.4	Rational and irrational self-talk	100

Foreword

Albert Ellis, the creator of Rational Emotive Behaviour Therapy (REBT), was someone I never met. However, having read his work extensively and discussed his ideas with people who have for the best part of a decade, it sometimes feels like I know him well. He seemed to have an unmistakable enthusiasm for psychotherapy, specifically to help people get better, not just feel better. To do this, he was dedicated to understanding as much as he could about the human condition from a variety of sources and disciplines, ranging from the ancient Stoics and Eastern philosophies to modern equivalents such as Aaron Beck. Above all else, however, he did it with an infectious humour and generosity (he held weekly group counselling sessions in New York that were available to everyone to make his approach open to all). I realize, as writing this, that these qualities could also be describing Dr Martin J. Turner.

I've known Martin for about a decade, having met him when he was delivering content on my MSc in applied sport psychology, and have been fortunate enough to have him as one of my PhD supervisors for half of that time. I got lucky. Not only is Martin one of the leading authorities in REBT, meaning you are in very safe hands reading this book, but he is also someone who, above all else, wants to help develop others' understanding of this subject. I have lost count of the number of messages and emails I've sent him requesting his thoughts on a paragraph I've just read or a comment he has made on my work, none of which have been ignored. Further, they are often met with a response that does not seem like a supervisor working with a student, but from a colleague, an equal. As Martin would say, we are "scientists in cahoots".

You will find that you are working with Martin as you progress through this book. Reflecting Ellis' openness to falsification and questioning, Martin presents the framework and central concepts of REBT in a manner that allows you to discover what rational thinking is but, importantly, what it is not. He will not tell you how to think, nor present evidence that has not been empirically tested, considered, and critiqued. This is invaluable given that we live in a world where, despite our modern conveniences, we are disturbed by events, others, and ourselves more than ever, as well as being exposed to any number of gurus who claim to have a silver bullet for our problems. Therefore, this book is timely.

Not only is the book of contemporary relevance, but it is also timeless. It is because we will all experience emotional disturbance that this book is of genuine value. In our podcast, *Rationally Speaking,* Martin and I frequently use examples from music, film, and sports to act as a vehicle through which to discuss REBT. We do this not only because, we hope, it is engaging but also because it demonstrates that anxiety, low-frustration tolerance, self-depreciation, and demandingness (e.g., irrationality) are part of the human condition. But humans are also powerful in that we can think about our thinking. It's just that we rarely (or effectively) contemplate how we may be creating or contributing to our own discomfort or how we can promote change. As you will see, the GABCDE framework provides the reader with a guide to helping themselves, with the ultimate goal of making the therapist redundant and empowering the individual.

I hope you enjoy reading about REBT and learning from Martin as much as I have and continue to do.

Stuart Carrington
March 2026
London

Acknowledgements

When I set out to create a more digestible version of my previous REBT book, I was at first dreading the thought of paring back vast amounts of text. As anyone who has worked with me on a paper will tell you, I am not good at losing words (!). But what this project has allowed me to do is get to the point with how we can apply REBT as practitioners. The essence of the larger text is still here in this book, and important details remain. But I have synthesized and made more concise these details, allowing myself to pursue less tangents and mount less meandering theoretical expeditions. I hope I have created a brief resource that practitioners can take off the shelf when they need some REBT inspiration.

I want to thank the many students, trainees, and professionals who have engaged with my work, and REBT more broadly. The notion that practitioners are out there using REBT with clients is sustaining and motivating. Thank you to the "REBTers" who challenge my thinking and to the wider REBT community for supporting what I am doing.

I also want to thank my colleagues for their support and encouragement, in particular Stuart Carrington, Nanaki J. Chadha, Jenni McArthur, Marc Jones, and Andrew Wood. I especially thank Stuart for providing the foreword to this text.

A big thank you goes to David Varley and Megan Smith at Routledge for their limitless support and assistance in this project.

Most importantly, I thank my wife Jayne, who surprisingly continues to entertain my REBT ramblings on a daily basis. As many practitioners working in performance settings know, our work is often uncertain, takes us all over the world, and can be all-consuming. So, I thank her for her support and patience over the years.

Praise for previous book, *The Rational Practitioner*

In this book Martin goes deep into REBT and excavates key elements that can be applied in sport and performance environments. As well as offering important theoretical clarifications, there is also a wealth of practitioner tools and techniques in the book. As a sport psychologist who utilises an REBT approach in my own practice, I'm always looking for resources to aid my consultancy practice. Martin's book is a keen addition to my library and one that will continue to guide my use of this important and powerful approach to behaviour change.

Dan Abrahams
Sport Psychologist

Sport psychology publications are too frequently characterised by ideas and approaches that are light on evidence and heavy on the superficial charm of buzzwords or personality. This is not one of those publications. It is both refreshing and reassuring to see the author dig deep into the rich history of psychotherapy, providing a sound philosophical and scientific rationale for the application of REBT to the field of sport and performance.

Dr Richard Bennett
Clinical Psychologist
Lecturer in the Centre for Applied Psychology at
The University of Birmingham
Co-author of *Acceptance and Commitment Therapy: 100 Key Points and Techniques* and *The Mindfulness and Acceptance Workbook for Self-esteem*

True to REBT's nature, Dr Turner adopts a no-nonsense and reality-based approach in articulating the practical application of REBT to sport and high-performance settings. A premier expert in the field of sport and exercise psychology, Dr Turner has been a forerunner in demonstrating the empirical support of REBT for athletes and performers. He has devoted his career to disseminating the evidence base of REBT for these populations. This book is a prodigious culmination of his life's work and is a must-read for sport and performance psychologists.

Dr Angela Breitmeyer
Associate Professor, Licensed Clinical Psychologist,
and Certified Mental Performance Consultant
Midwestern University, Glendale, Arizona

This book is an informative and invaluable resource for practitioners who are interested in applying REBT within the sport and performance setting. The book comprehensively brings together the theoretical underpinning and evidence-based practice of REBT. The author sharing ideas from his own applied practice and using quotes and media references throughout the text makes it an engaging and stimulating read.

Dr Nanaki J. Chadha
Sport and Exercise Psychologist

Martin J. Turner provides thorough and fascinating insights into the approach of Rational Emotive Behaviour Therapy (REBT) in this practitioner guide. Drawing on his vast wealth of knowledge and practical experiences of REBT in sport, this book is indispensable for anyone looking to fully understand REBT theory, explore technical components of REBT and practically use REBT successfully when working with clients. Everyone who is interested in performance should read it.

Helen Davis
Director and Sport Psychologist at Think.Believe.Perform
England Women's Rugby team – The Red Roses

Martin J. Turner is one of the leading figures in REBT, and this book displays exactly why. This book serves as a complete guide for using REBT as a toolkit, and encapsulates the whole process of REBT from beginning to end. This book is fantastically well-written, easy to understand, memorable, and brutally honest in its intentions and in REBT's bounds as a therapeutic framework. This book will be a landmark in the field of sport and performance psychology for many years to come.

Muhammad Saqib Deen
Performance Psychology Consultant

Driven by utilitarianism, Martin J. Turner draws on over a decade of experience and research to offer populous pearls of REBT wisdom. This belongs on the desk of all practitioners who have a vested interest in facilitating deep solutions for performance issues.

Dr Faye F. Didymus
Reader in Sport and Performance Psychology
Leeds Beckett University

As an applied practitioner in elite sport and business I have found REBT a hugely valuable and impactful approach when working with high performing individuals and teams. The principles, frameworks and language consistently resonate powerfully with those operating in a performance environment who connect to the ideas of working with a more rational mindset. I am extremely excited that Martin has been able to consolidate his learning and experience into this fantastic guide. I thoroughly recommend it as a wonderful companion for anyone looking to learn about and apply REBT in their work.

Dr Joseph Dixon
Sport and Exercise and Occupational Psychologist
Staffordshire University, Coventry City FC

The book provides a forensic and comprehensive examination of the key theory, frameworks and technical components central to the REBT approach, and an effective guide for those who wish to contribute to the growing application of REBT in sport and performance settings. In my professional lead role as an educator and trainer of Sport and Exercise Psychologists, the book represents an extremely valuable resource for those applied practitioners wishing to develop the knowledge and skills required to effectively use REBT in their service delivery with clients.

Dr Martin Eubank
LJMU Professional Doctorate Programme Director and
BPS Qualification Lead in Sport and Exercise Psychology

Learning to become a sport psychologist is like picking up shards of a smashed antique jug. As you discuss and grow with others in the field, you slowly piece it together to develop your practice. Learning REBT fully is like being the person who has the vase and uses it to pour out the wine of rational truth for your clients. Dr Turner's book is of immense value for his robust depth of knowledge on REBT. I would prefer for it to have existed when I began my career providing sport psychology to Olympians and Paralympians. Every day we accept reality and are undisturbed by it. Frequently though, things occur and we become disturbed. In sport we face failure, injury, setbacks, sometimes even death, amidst the harsh existence of life. It is within those most difficult of cases where the most robust and accessible approaches will prevail, and REBT serves these challenges well. In a field that promotes positivity and happiness as the end goal, REBT cuts through the nonsense to leave humans in control of their reality.

Hugh J. Gilmore
Sport Psychologist with British Weightlifting and British Athletics
Podium Psychology

Martin J. Turner has achieved something special with this book. By combining his sophisticated understanding of REBT and the unique demands coming from the world of sports, he offers great insight and practical solutions that unlock optimal performance. Sport is a microcosm of life. We learn so much from participating in the game. Dr Turner's "Rational Practitioner" book helps all of us discover philosophies and applied answers that can help us navigate the complexities of life in addition to sport.

Dr Scott Goldman
Clinical and Sport Psychologist who has been embedded
with multiple NFL, NBA, MLB, and NCAA teams

Sport culture has for too long propagated a host of incredibly unhelpful attitudes and perspectives around what it means to be an athlete and the inherent value of winning. So few coaches and others in supporting roles are conscious of the perspectives or beliefs that could be dramatically holding back their athletes. REBT is a powerful concept to bring into performance sport because it provides a solid foundational mindset, more closely aligned to the reality of any situation, from which athletes can build on and achieve their potential. Elite sport is crying out for a healthier approach;

one that does not break down or burnout its participants so consistently. A more widespread understanding of the theory and practice of REBT would be a vital part of that healthier approach.

Laurence Cassøe Halsted
Director of Mentoring, The True Athlete Project

Martin is the go-to person for all things REBT in sport. In this book he unassumingly provides valuable insight for both the REBT novice and expert; a valuable addition to any sport and exercise psychologist's bookshelf.

Dr Jennifer Hobson
Sport and Exercise Psychologist

This book provides an invaluable resource for trainee practitioners, experienced consultants and those with an interest in a particular application of psychology within sport and other high performance contexts. The book breaks down the REBT approach into meaningful and interconnected components and guides the reader in a clear and coherent manner to encourage effective use of it within applied practice.

Dr Tim Holder
Senior Lecturer in Sport and Exercise Psychology
University of Winchester

I have found REBT and some of its key tenets to be hugely valuable as I develop as a practitioner. In learning about the theory I have often looked to Martin's writing in the area, and can personally endorse his simple and down to earth way of breaking down key concepts and arming you with actionable tools to take into practice.

Pete Jackson
Sport and Exercise Psychologist (BPS)
London

It can be hard to recognise the value of adopting an REBT approach until one is simultaneously fully immersed in its theories and responding to the complex needs of clients who brave high-risk contexts. Until recently a developing sport and performance psychology practitioner may have felt vulnerable relying so heavily on an approach which seemed so un-tested in our context. Dr Turner's important book, and ever-growing contribution to our understanding of REBT in performance settings, provides practitioners with a much-desired navigation system for applying one of the most efficient and effective approaches to stress and emotion management that there is.

Dr Jenni McArthur
Performance Psychologist

The application of REBT in sport and exercise settings is relatively new and rapidly growing. It is the toolkit that practitioners can use to help athletes make sense their thoughts, actions, and feelings. A great deal of the work stems from Dr Martin J. Turner and this book with so many fascinating, insightful and practically useful chapters will be an asset to practitioners and students alike.

Dr Andrew Lane
Professor of Sport Psychology
University of Wolverhampton

As applied sport psychologists working within high performance environments, we are charged with deciding which approaches and frameworks we learn and utilise with clients. In *The Rational Practitioner*, Martin offers a comprehensive account of the REBT approach, and the GABCDE framework found within it, to working in performance settings. Martin links REBT with ideas and techniques common to sport psychology, helping REBT to be seen as a broad approach to working with clients, rather than a niche psychotherapy only for clinical usage. Alongside much theoretical detail, Martin offers many practical ideas and concepts for practitioners to use in their work, making the book useful for applied psychologists working in the real world.

Rebecca Levett
Sport and Exercise Psychologist
Sporting Success

This is a very useful and practical book. It is a welcome resource that I enthusiastically recommend. Martin's engaging writing style, suitable demonstration of the effectiveness of REBT as an approach should have a wide appeal to practitioners of all disciplines who support participants involved in sport and high performance settings. It is an information-packed and thought provoking read and will no doubt be trusted reference

Andy McCann
Professor of Psychology, Human Performance Practitioner
Manchester Metropolitan University

Dr Martin J. Turner's accessible, engaging, and scholarly text about practising Rational Emotive Behaviour Therapy in sport and high performance instructs as it enlightens. His is the best style of practising guide: it knits its extensive scholarship gracefully into each sentence, it presents concepts and practice in sensible and measured lots, and what sits on these pages permeated from years of exceptional scholarship and practical experience.

Dr Paul McCarthy
Senior Lecturer in Applied Psychology
Glasgow Caledonian University

REBT can be a useful approach to help performers perceive stressful situations as a challenge. Interestingly, this can be done by reflecting on the beliefs behind the demands, and if these are irrational, REBT can be useful in lowering the weight of the demands, through moving away from the "musts". It also helps to draw in the resources to help cope with the demands of the situation, through considering how to work towards healthy emotions. As such, this text is an invaluable resource for practitioners who are working with stress and emotions in athletes.

Dr Carla Meijen
Assistant Professor in Organizational and Sport Psychology
University of Amsterdam

This book is a much needed delve into the value of REBT in sport. For researchers and practitioners alike, it gives a detailed overview of the key theoretical underpinnings and how to use it in practice. It is a must read for all those with an interest in working with or using REBT.

Dr Robert Morris
Associate Professor in Sport
University of Stirling

For those of us researching and consulting in this field, Martin is acknowledged as an academic practitioner who has developed into a World Leading Expert on REBT within the sport setting. I am, therefore, delighted that Martin has translated his knowledge and experience into this accessible text. What follows is a user-friendly guide that will help those involved in sport understand and utilise an evidence-based and flexible approach to emotion management.

Professor Rich Neil
Cardiff Metropolitan University

The Rational Practitioner is a very welcome and timely contribution to the field, providing fourteen chapters offering insights and evidence-based discussion. Dr Martin J. Turner's new book aims to inform the work of psychologists and is also essential reading for anyone interested in learning more about the field of Rational Emotive Behaviour Therapy in the contexts of sport and performance.

Dr Siobhain O'Riordan
Chartered Coaching Psychologist

This book is another great contribution by Dr Martin J. Turner on the use of REBT in sport. Not only does Martin provide readers with a rich insight into the theory and implementation of REBT within sport settings, but he does so in a witty, engaging, and accessible way. This book is a must-have resource for any practitioner looking to expand their knowledge and practice of REBT.

Dr Erin Prior
Lecturer in Psychology
Loughborough University

For anyone interested in learning more about the REBT approach, irrespective of their level of practitioner and/or academic and/or research experience, this text is an absolute must. From raising awareness to the theoretical underpinning of REBT, the text comprehensively works through key research contributions and integrates the implications for applied practice. Written in a manner that encourages critical thinking, the text includes many examples that will support reflections and future work using the approach, and perhaps even lead to some new "Effective beliefs" about the approach.

Dr Richard Thelwell
Professor of Applied Sport Psychology
University of Portsmouth

The notion that helpful thoughts and actions don't have to be overtly positivity is a "game-changer" to many athletes. This book and its exploration of the use REBT in sport and performance settings is in many ways a great reflection of the author – rich and deep in knowledge, with tangible simplicity at the fore. The principles of REBT in a wider sense provide a great fit to sporting practice – after all, the things we fear or avoid are all part of life's performance.

Betsy Tuffrey
Sport and Exercise Psychologist, Seed Psychology Ltd.

I have been fortunate enough to work with Martin in a business setting and see the benefit of applying REBT to a group going through redundancy. The group benefited enormously to reframe a situation they saw as a "disaster" into a potential opportunity. As a result, all members of the group were able to move on into new roles with their confidence levels enhanced rather than reduced.

Roy White
Ex-Vice President Human Resources, Sony Europe

Introduction

Why does this book exist? In writing my previous book *The Rational Practitioner,* my aim was to provide a very comprehensive portrayal of Rational Emotive Behaviour Therapy (REBT). I wanted to get across the deep and rich complexity of REBT while also providing applied tools for practitioners to adopt in their own work. I believe I succeeded in my aim (if I do say so myself). But not everybody wants or needs a protracted account of REBT. Some practitioners want to cut to the chase. Indeed, one of the strengths of REBT is that it is simultaneously simple and complex. It is possible to apply REBT without knowing the depths of REBT theory. In the current book, I provide a briefer but no less accurate account of REBT theory and practice. I do this for three main reasons:

- To supply REBT practitioners with a go-to resource that they can dip in and out of for REBT guidance
- To supply neophytes with an easy to digest portrayal of REBT to stimulate their interest and use of REBT
- To supplement the longer Rational Practitioner book with a briefer, punchier account of the work.

I needed to write *The Rational Practitioner*. I needed to write it, probably more than anybody needed to read it (!). I needed to write it because *I* needed to read it, and it wasn't currently written – so I had to write it. I know this is like the ouroboros (snake eating its own tail). But I learned many valuable lessons while writing it and then reading it. I learned about the depth of REBT both psychologically and philosophically. I learned about my own capacity to understand and communicate REBT, and relatedly, I learned that there is a lot that can be written about REBT. I also learned what the most important features of the book are in helping readers to apply REBT in their practice. I learned, from readers, what a distillation of the book might look like. As such, *this* book is leaner, more concise, but no less instructive.

I start this book as I mean to go on. In this first chapter I offer a brief introduction to the book. In the 1950s Albert Ellis conceived Rational Emotive Behaviour Therapy (REBT), then called Rational Therapy (RT). In recent years, really since the 2000s (although there are of course many earlier examples) the work reporting the use of REBT has been rapidly growing. This book is an amalgamation of what

DOI: 10.4324/9781003508472-1

I have learned about the application of REBT, not only from conducting empirical research, but also by making REBT the centre of the psychology support I have provided clients. This book offers a flexible approach to applied psychology that underpins the pursuit and fulfilment of human potential, using REBT as its foundation.

The road to fulfilment, however you define it, is of course decorated by (often unavoidable) adversity. As such, this book has essentially one basic guiding principle: *do not make things worse*. To elaborate, do not think, act, and feel in ways that turn adversity into catastrophe. Don't think, act, and feel in ways that facilitate self-destruction and that self-sabotage goal pursuit. Of course, facing adversity may generate unpleasant and unwanted emotion, but do not unnecessarily and foolishly propagate dysfunctional and maladaptive emotions. Things can get bad, really bad. And we have the capacity to make things worse, much worse. So, this book is underpinned, firstly, by the philosophy of not making things worse by how we think, act, and feel. *Only then* can you try to make things better. This is done by thinking, acting, and feeling in ways that are constructive for goal attainment. *Constructive* does not mean *positive* in valence. This book is not about positive thinking or optimism. Rather, this book is about helping people to deal with the world as it is, rather than how they would like it to be. Therefore, and crucially, by learning to *not make things worse*, we can *make things better*. Of course, not making things worse and making things better are potentially interrelated or interacting ideas, but they are definitionally different. In this book, I certainly construe REBT as a remedial approach to helping people deal with adversity, but I also, *and equally*, present REBT as a proactive approach to helping clients fulfil their potential.

> We had better accept what is going on (WIGO) in the world as "reality," even when we don't like it and are trying to change it.
>
> -Ellis (1996a, p. 26)

Against the backdrop of stress and adversity that permeates daily life, an approach to psychology that promotes health and function, but is accepting and acknowledging of the demanding and often adverse nature of life, is valuable. Through REBT, we treat the world as it is, not how we would like it to be. REBT is not for fantasists or blind optimists. We help clients to develop reality-based life philosophies, rather than fictional narratives. We don't offer delusions. We tether the client to the reality they are familiar with, in which negative emotion is inescapable, inevitable, anticipated, and normal, as well as being potentially advantageous, often serving important functions in the pursuit of a meaningful life.

In REBT we assume (correctly) that life is difficult and demanding, and that human beings are limited and thus will experience suffering, but have the capacity to cope with life's challenges through purposeful choice. William James (considered the father of American psychology) said, "the greatest weapon against stress is our ability to choose one thought over another" and I agree. We have the choice to believe one thing over another, after first engaging critically in what we believe as beings capable of scientific thought and metacognition (thinking about thinking).

This idea of thinking about thinking is vital for critical thought, and critical engagement with our environment, and is obviously important in life. It is also fundamental to the practice of REBT.

So, REBT is especially applicable to human beings because it recognizes that life is adverse and that human beings are fallible, and then works to enhance adaptive function under such stressful circumstances amidst our limitations. It points the finger *inwardly* first with regards to emotional control, and *outwardly* second (or not at all depending on the circumstances). What can *I* do to manage my emotions? *Then*, how could the environment be enhanced in order to help me manage my emotions? If I can manage my thoughts, my emotions, my behaviours, then I might be able to attain some of my goals and forthrightly move towards the fulfilment of my potential.

Therapy?

REBT delivered non-clinically, for example in work and performance environments, has been called "Smarter Thinking" (Turner, 2014) and or REB Coaching (REBC; Breitmeyer & Turner, 2018). This is done in part to reduce the clinical connotations associated with "therapy". When I am engaging clients in REBT, I am not doing therapy. I am trained in psychotherapies as a practitioner psychologist, I am registered with the Health Care Professions Council (HCPC), but I am not clinically trained. I am using a therapeutic framework to aid clients as they deal with the ubiquitous vicissitudes and adversity of life. I, as a practitioner, should not shy away from this. Training in psychotherapies, like REBT, furnishes me with incredibly useful frameworks and techniques that can help clients outside of the clinical milieu, not just remedially, but proactively.

The structure of this book

In the book you are reading, I front-load REBT theory by outlining what REBT is (Chapter 1), before moving on to the core technical components of REBT. This includes the underpinning framework of REBT (Chapter 2), detailed content around each aspect of the framework (Chapters 4 to 10), and the key practitioner-client factors to consider for successful REBT (Chapter 3). Within these chapters I also cover assessment and intervention details, but the key intervention content appears when we get to disputation and effective new beliefs (Chapters 9 and 10). I include professional practice guidance for the use of REBT. I use applied examples throughout the book as illustrations of REBT in use, but I never name or intimate individuals I have worked with, and thus, any client names in this book are pseudonyms.

A final word

In this book, I do not present REBT as the only way, or as a panacea, for practice, and my role is not to convince you the reader to use REBT, but to sincerely set out the framework and applied utility of REBT for practitioners as lucidly as I can. REBT is not the only approach I use, nonetheless, whether it is a strategy for self-care, a one-to-one approach to helping clients, or a psycho-educational framework to deliver with leaders, REBT theory and practice have afforded me a meaningful and comprehensive approach to understanding, explaining, encouraging, and propagating the fulfilment of human potential.

1 Rational emotive behaviour therapy

What is Rational Emotive Behaviour Therapy?

Rational Emotive Behaviour Therapy (REBT) was developed by Albert Ellis in the 1950s (it was called RT, then RET, now REBT; Ellis, 1995) and represents the first of the cognitive behavioural therapies (CBTs). REBT is a second-wave CBT that holds a firm place within the CBT family of psychotherapies, predicated on the blending of cognitive- and behaviour-based elements (Bennett & Oliver, 2019). The central goal of REBT is to help clients to improve their functioning by means of introspective identification and direct challenging of the maladaptive beliefs that interfere with their ability to pursue and fulfil their goals (Caserta et al., 2010). In other words, in REBT we help clients to first understand their self-limiting beliefs, and to then address these beliefs forthrightly. Ellis (1988) expressed three main tenets of REBT: "being aware of your dysfunctional and Irrational Beliefs, cognitively-emotionally-behaviorally Disputing them, and arriving at Effective New Philosophies or Rational Coping Philosophies" (p. 10). The same goals could characterize other CBTs, but REBT is distinct from other CBTs (such as cognitive therapy, CT; Beck, 1976, and acceptance and commitment therapy, ACT; Hayes et al., 2013), due to its emphasis on rational (flexible, non-extreme, and logical) and irrational (rigid, extreme, and illogical) beliefs as key cognitive mediators between a situation (or inferences about a situation) and affective and behavioural reactivity (see Turner et al., 2020a for a comparison of CBTs). But while REBT is distinguished from other CBTs owing to its specific focus on irrational and rational beliefs, the practice of REBT does not reflect a blinkered obsession with beliefs and on the contrary can incorporate many cognitive, emotive, and behavioural methods found in other CBTs.

The primary form of REBT is known as "specific", "preferential", or "elegant" REBT, in which the client is enabled to weaken their rigid and extreme beliefs and develop and strengthen flexible and non-extreme beliefs. The secondary form of REBT is known as "general" or "inelegant" REBT, in which a large variety of cognitive, emotive, and behavioural techniques are applied, and in which belief change is not necessarily the main focus (see Dryden & David, 2008, for a full discussion). Thus, general (inelegant) REBT includes a variety of cognitive-emotive-behavioural

DOI: 10.4324/9781003508472-2

methods (Lazarus, 1995), not just disputation of irrational beliefs, and as such is synonymous with a broad understanding of what CBT is and does (Ellis, 1977).

Where REBT becomes more distinct from CBT per se is in its specific (elegant) form, where the irrational, deep-seated fundamental, beliefs become more of the focus, alongside a variety of cognitive-emotive-behavioural methods (Ellis, 1977). In other words, general REBT offers a broad cognitive-emotive-behavioural approach which *does not necessarily* address the deep-seated fundamental irrational beliefs, while specific REBT can still offer a broad cognitive-emotive-behavioural approach, but it *does necessarily* address the deep-seated fundamental irrational beliefs. So, specific REBT "especially (but never solely) stresses the achievement of a profound cognitive or philosophic change in clients' basic assumptions, especially their absolutistic demanding, musterbatory, irrational ways of viewing themselves, others, and the world" (Ellis, 1977, p. 74). While the main thrust of the current book is specific, elegant, REBT, I do recognize and incorporate general, inelegant, REBT in aspects of this book, because as Ellis recognized himself in 1977, REBT is frequently done inelegantly (i.e., general REBT) and REBT should not be defined monolithically.

REBT's distinctiveness is also achieved by its inclusion of a binary theory of emotional distress (BTED; e.g., Ellis, 1994), in which not all negative (valenced) emotions are considered unhealthy or targets for change (DiGiuseppe et al., 2014). In brief, in the BTED, in response to adversity rational beliefs beget healthy negative emotions (HNEs; e.g., concern [healthy anxiety], sadness, healthy anger), whereas irrational beliefs beget unhealthy negative emotions (UNEs; e.g., anxiety [unhealthy anxiety], depression, unhealthy anger: Dryden, 2008, Ellis, 1994). HNEs are functional and adaptive for goal attainment, and UNEs are dysfunctional and maladaptive (for a fuller critical discussion, see Turner et al., 2018a, 2019a). Therefore, REBT does not explicitly aim to foster positive (valenced) emotion and does not accept mere symptom removal (Ellis, 1977), but works towards healthy emotions and away from unhealthy emotions, more interested in function than valence, *getting* better rather than just *feeling* better (Ellis, 2001).

REBT is perhaps most different to other CBTs due to its emphasis on rational and irrational beliefs. There are four core rational beliefs and four core irrational beliefs. Rational beliefs comprise a primary belief known as "preferences", and three secondary beliefs known as frustration tolerance (FT), anti-awfulizing, and unconditional self/other/world acceptance (USA/UOA/UWA). Irrational beliefs comprise a primary belief known as "demandingness", and three secondary beliefs known as frustration intolerance (FI), awfulizing, and depreciation (or global evaluation; GE). The primary and secondary structure of beliefs in REBT is known as the REBT-I Model (DiLorenzo et al., 2007; Turner et al., 2019b). While demandingness appears to be part of a primary appraisal process, awfulizing, FI, and depreciation appear to be part of a secondary appraisal process (e.g., David et al., 2002) and as such may be more closely linked to specific emotional outcomes.

Rational beliefs are flexible, non-extreme, logical, and functional, and in contrast, irrational beliefs are rigid, extreme, illogical, and dysfunctional. Unsurprisingly then, given that irrational beliefs are non-sensical and underpin UNEs, one of the chief aims of REBT is to help clients undermine and weaken irrational beliefs, and develop and strengthen rational beliefs, which are sensical and underpin HNEs. REBT is predicated on the axioms that (1) cognitions can be identified and measured, (2) cognitions play a central role in psychological functioning, (3) irrational cognitions can be weakened in favour of rational cognitions, and (4) this irrational-rational transition abets functional emotional, cognitive, and behavioural responses in keeping with personal goals (David et al., 2010).

The core concepts of REBT, that of rational and irrational beliefs, the BTED, and cognitive mediation, are captured and abstracted within the GABCDE framework, illustrated in Figure 1.1. The GABCDE framework portrays the overarching theory of REBT, illustrates the aetiology of well-being and ill-being, and guides client assessment and intervention work. It presents important steps for the practitioner-client work that if not approached properly can undercut the effectiveness of the work. It is also used as a way to teach clients about the relationships between events (and inferences about events), their beliefs, and their emotional and behavioural experiences. If clients present with irrational beliefs (iBs) that, in response to adverse events (A), manifest to block or impede their goals (G), they are likely to experience unhealthy negative emotions (UNEs) as a consequence (C). Thus, clients are encouraged to rigorously dispute (D) and challenge these irrational beliefs (iBs), and then rational beliefs (rBs) are encouraged, challenged, and reinforced (E) to help the client experience healthy emotions and adaptive behaviours. The GABCDE framework proposes that irrational beliefs underpin emotional disturbance, and that weakening irrational beliefs and strengthening more adaptive rational beliefs better enable individuals to reach their goals and to live more rewarding lives (Browne et al., 2010).

Importantly, while irrational beliefs are at the centre of REBT theory and practice, it is of course recognized that adverse events are important for emotional

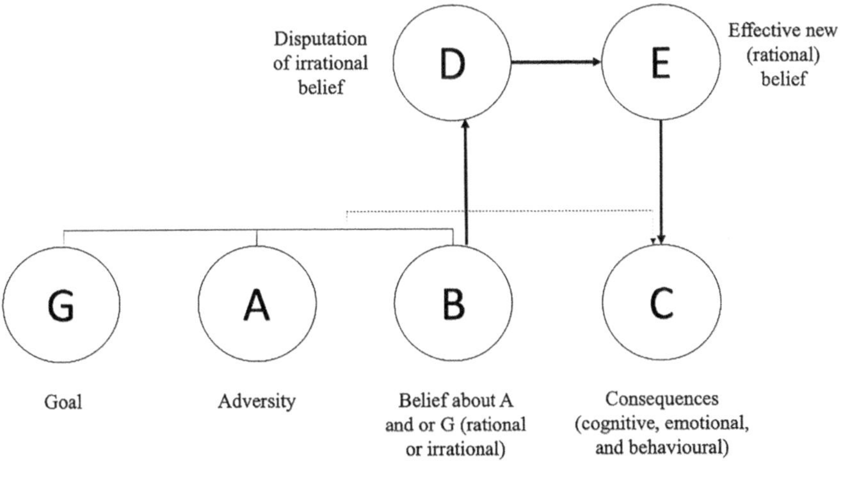

Figure 1.1 The GABCDE framework of REBT

responding; AxB=C (Dryden, 2012a; Ellis, 2002a). Indeed, while irrational beliefs largely underpin UNEs at C, "REBT theorists are careful to avoid saying that B causes C" (Dryden, 2012a, p. 39) and REBT holds that "cognitions do not by themselves cause emotional disturbance" (Ellis, 1977, p. 75). The present author is not innocent of B-C causation language in his earlier works. It is important to understand that the aetiology of emotion is complex and multifaceted and includes biological and environmental influences. But for REBT, cognition is considered to be the most important source of disturbance in most humans, most of the time (Ellis, 1977).

Ellis was not so much of an active researcher as he was a theorist and psychotherapist, and there is a continuing need to study REBT empirically (Dryden & David, 2008). However, through the 1990s and 2000s various reviews and meta-analyses have been conducted that capture the research that has been undertaken in REBT (David et al., 2018, 2021; Engels et al., 1993; Gonzalez et al., 2004; Jordana et al., 2023; King et al., 2024; Lyons & Woods, 1991; Priyadarshini & Jose, 2025; Trip et al., 2007), both at a practical and theoretical level. It is worth noting that in the field of REBT, sport is considered to be a dominant domain (Priyadarshini & Jose, 2025), and what we are learning about REBT through sport is important for the field of REBT per se. From the first REBT in sport paper (Bernard, 1985) to our very recent work (Elvins et al., 2025), there is some agreement that REBT is an effective approach to sport psychology, evidenced across various sports, levels, and countries. For reviews concerning REBT in sport, readers are directed to Jordana et al. (2023), King et al. (2024), and Turner (2016b, 2022). The applied REBT research will continue to grow as more trainees and postgraduate practitioner-researchers discover REBT and begin to test it in their own practice. In 2022 a special issue in the *Journal of Rational-Emotive and Cognitive-Behavioral Therapy* brought together studies from across the REBT community. Therefore, our understanding of how REBT can be applied in settings such sport, work, education, military, and health is becoming richer and more nuanced, paving the way for those entering into these settings to use REBT in their practice supported by growing evidence.

Summary

The study and application of REBT will continue to grow and possibly change beyond the horizon of this book. As Ellis said in 1979, "Nothing is sacred – including RE[B]T!" The literature concerning REBT is vibrant and diverse. However, the growth of REBT literature, especially papers that have offered applied developments and innovations, and therefore there is a constant need to revise and expand REBT practice guidelines. The current book offers a contemporary account of how REBT can be applied, taking what I have learned from the emergent research published in the last decade, and from my continual practice of REBT across many contexts. In the current book I aim to provide a state-of-the-art but brief guide to the application of REBT.

2 The GABCDE framework

Albert Ellis was, perhaps obviously given his role in REBT, very skilled in laying out the core theory of REBT in this written and spoken works. The core framework of REBT is the GABCDE framework, with GABC really underpinning the theory of psychological well-being in REBT and also guiding how assessment is structured during client work. For example, Ellis (1994) states:

> When people have their goals and values (G's) of remaining alive and making themselves happy, and when activating events or activating experiences (A's) block and thwart these goals, they have the choice of making themselves feel healthily or self-helpingly sorry, regretful, frustrated, or disappointed at point C, their emotional consequences; or they can (consciously or unconsciously) choose to make themselves unhealthily or neurotically panicked, depressed, horrified, enraged, self-hating, or self-pitying at C.
>
> (p. 17)

This chapter is about the core framework that underpins REBT theory and practice. A clear articulation of the GABCDE framework is necessary if we are to fully explain how REBT is practiced because the framework informs most of what we do in practice (both implicitly and explicitly). Also, this chapter provides the foundation for everything else that follows in this book, since the content of the book is fully aligned with the GABCDE framework. In this chapter I outline the GABCDE framework, cover some of its Stoic origins, align it with prominent emotion and emotion regulation theory, and detail techniques and strategies that can be used to bring the GABCDE framework to life in practice. Put plainly, the GABCDE framework (Figure 2.1) describes the aetiology of psychological disturbance, and psychological health, and guides client assessment and intervention work within REBT. As such, it is fundamental to REBT.

As can be seen in Figure 2.1, G, A, and B coalesce to influence C. In specific (elegant) REBT, D is applied to B, giving rise to E, which promotes a new C. The GABCDE is composed of:

G – *G*oals
A – *A*dversity (or *A*ctivating Event)

DOI: 10.4324/9781003508472-3

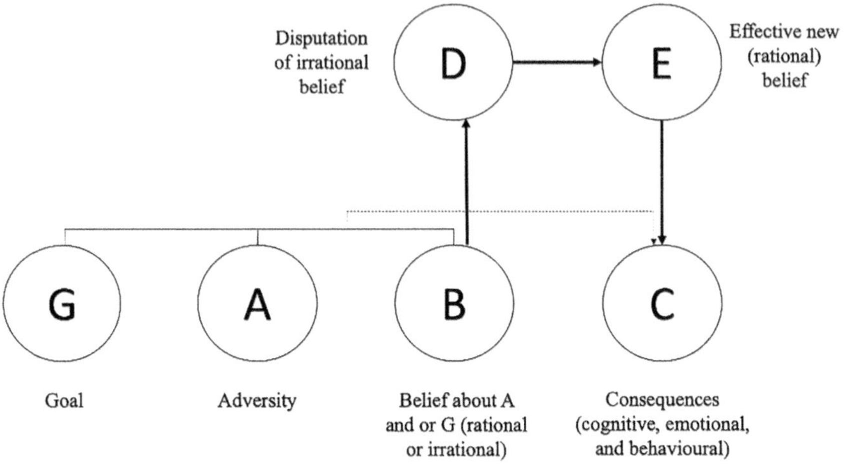

Figure 2.1 Diagrammatic representation of the GABCDE framework. The dotted line between GAB and C reflects pre-REBT and the move to D and E from B reflects the REBT process

B – Rational and Irrational *B*eliefs (rBs and iBs)
C – Cognitive, Emotional, and Behavioural *C*onsequences (UNE or HNE)
D – *D*isputation
E – *E*ffective New Beliefs

Goals (G)

Preferences and desires to survive, to assuage unnecessary pain, to be fulfilled (fundamental goals; FG), to be satisfied alone, socially, intimately, informationally, educationally, vocationally, economically, and recreationally (primary goals; PG), to be reasonable, logical, and successful in solving and mastering life problems and meaningful tasks, experiencing new and stimulating things, and being stable and secure in work and social life (Ellis, 1994). Importantly, Gs are not "needs", and rationality should be in the service of these Gs (Nelson-Jones, 2006). Importantly, Gs help contextualize Adversity (A) (Crawford & Ellis, 1989).

Adversity (A)

Unfortunate and undesirable occurrences that interfere with the attainment of Gs (Ellis, 1994; Shea, 2016), and are ubiquitous, copious, and unquantifiable, because As can be concrete or "real", can be entirely fictional (imagined or fabricated), but are usually inferential, reflecting a perception of something that has happened (or could/will happen). Dryden (2017) defines "As" as the aspects of the situation that the person focusses on and evaluates. Importantly, by hindering Gs, As help to give rise to negative emotion.

Beliefs (rational or irrational) (B)

Assumptions, attitudes, idea, rules, philosophies, ways of seeing the self, others, and the world, patterns of thinking (schema) that can be rational and or irrational. Specifically, rational beliefs are "beliefs that are logical, and/or have empirical support, and/or are pragmatic" and irrational beliefs are "beliefs that are illogical, and/or do not have empirical support, and/or are nonpragmatic" (Ellis et al., 2010, p. 3). Rational beliefs comprise a primary belief known as "preferences" and three secondary beliefs known as frustration tolerance (FT), anti-awfulizing, and unconditional self/other/world acceptance (USA/UOA/UWA). Irrational beliefs comprise a primary belief known as "demandingness" and three secondary beliefs known as frustration intolerance (FI), awfulizing, and depreciation (or global evaluation; GE). Rational beliefs are usually self-enhancing (Dryden, 2017) and often underpin healthy negative emotions (HNEs) (DiGiuseppe et al., 2014) and thus facilitate (or do not debilitate) goal attainment (Wilson, 2010). In contrast, irrational beliefs are usually self-defeating (Dryden, 2017) and often underpin unhealthy negative emotions (UNEs) (DiGiuseppe et al., 2014), and as such are usually unhelpful in pursuing, and inconsistent with accomplishing, one's long-term goals (Maultsby, 1975). As it is the development and enhancement of human functioning that is at the centre of REBT, rational beliefs are encouraged (promoted, reinforced, strengthened) and irrational beliefs are discouraged (challenge, weakened).

Consequences (C)

The cognitions, emotions, and behaviours arising from the interaction between Gs, As, and Bs. Cs can be healthy (healthy negative emotions; HNEs), whereby they are functional, adaptive, and appropriate, or Cs can be unhealthy (unhealthy negative emotions; UNEs), whereby they are dysfunctional, maladaptive, and inappropriate. Healthy Cs are self-enhancing, leading to constructive behaviour that aids goal (G) attainment, while unhealthy Cs are self-defeating, leading to unconstructive behaviour that interferes with goal (G) attainment (Dryden, 2022).

Disputation (D)

A collaborative (client-practitioner) and Socratic argument, or debate, applied systematically and rigorously, focussed on challenging client Bs in order to instigate a philosophic shift from irrationality to rationality. Disputation (D) largely applies logical-empirical methods of science (Dryden & Branch, 2008). Typical arguments include empirical (true or false?), logical (sensical or nonsensical?), and pragmatic (helpful or unhelpful?) questioning, where the veracity, logic, and utility of the Bs is challenged. Both irrational and rational beliefs are subject to Disputation (D) so that irrational beliefs can be understood to be false, illogical, and unhelpful, and rational beliefs can be understood to be true, logical, and helpful (for goal attainment). Clients should learn to independently dispute their Bs in the long-term, not just dispute the specific Bs relevant to the current client-practitioner work.

Effective New Beliefs (E)

The defining, development, strengthening of, and long-term commitment to, rational beliefs. Rational beliefs are encouraged while irrational beliefs are discouraged, and cognitive, emotive, and behavioural strategies are meaningfully rehearsed and enacted upon in service of deepening (strengthen their conviction in) the rational beliefs and applying rationality independently over the life course. The client is supported in integrating the rational beliefs, and the notion of rationality, into their lives via an ongoing commitment to the effective new rational beliefs (E).

Rational versus irrational GABC

As can be seen in Figure 2.2, if clients hold irrational beliefs (iB) that, in response to adverse events (A) manifest to block or impede their goals (G), they are likely to experience UNEs (C). Then, as can be seen in Figure 2.3, if clients hold rational beliefs (rBs) that, in response to adverse events (A) manifest to aid their goals (G), they are likely to experience HNEs (C). Thus, clients are encouraged to rigorously dispute (D) these irrational beliefs (iBs), and rational beliefs (rBs) are then encouraged and reinforced (E) to help the client experience HNEs at (C). Simply, irrational beliefs underpin UNEs (e.g., David et al., 2002), and rational beliefs underpin HNEs (e.g., Oltean & David, 2018). In basic terms, the GABCDE framework portrays a cognitive approach to emotion and behaviour, which assumes that consequences (C) are at least in part cognitively penetrable (David et al., 2004, 2010). Thus, REBT subscribes to a cognitive model (e.g., Dobson & Dozois, 2010) in which cognitive change is important for treatment.

The Stoic undergirding of the GABCDE framework

> Where did the GABCDE framework come from? The GABCDE framework is clearly underpinned in part by Stoic doctrines, particularly the philosophy and teachings of Epictetus. The Stoicism of Epictetus in particular is clearly reflected in the GABCDE framework and REBT at large. When formally introducing the theory of REBT in 1962, Ellis himself wrote:

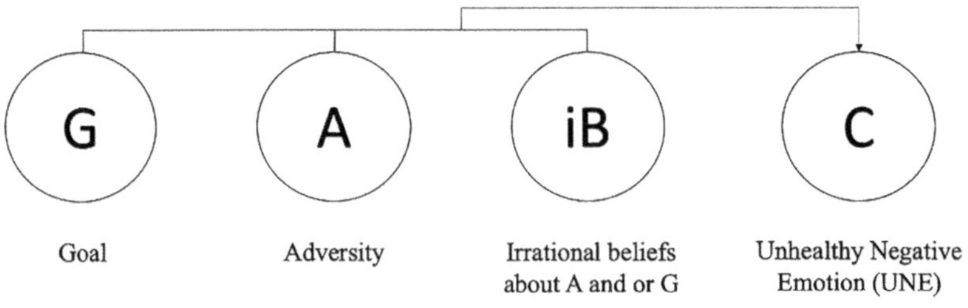

Figure 2.2 Diagrammatic representation of *irrational* GABC

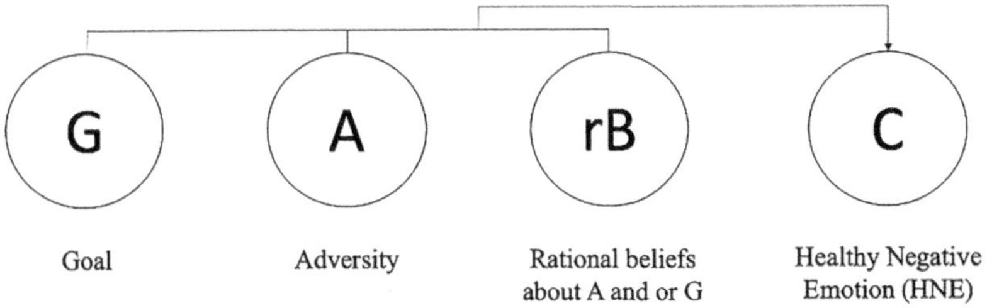

Figure 2.3 Diagrammatic representation of *rational* GABC

> Many of the principles incorporated in the theory of rational-emotive psychotherapy are not new; some of them, in fact, were originally stated several thousand years ago, especially by the Greek and Roman Stoic philosophers (such as Epictetus and Marcus Aurelius).
>
> (Ellis, 1962, p. 35)

Ellis adopts the Stoic idea that reason and rationality are fundamental to being and also that a "good" life is underpinned by the expression of healthy (functional) emotions. Ellis also aligns REBT with the Stoic notion of cognitive mediation, an idea that emerged more formally in the cognitive revolution of the 1950s (Ruggiero et al., 2018). Cognitive mediators are defined as "mental processes or activities that take place between the initial occurrence of a stimulus and the subsequent related response" (Alegria & Cameron, 2020, p. 496). Cognitive mediation is foundational to CBTs as well as to the advancement of emotion regulation sciences (e.g., Gross, 1998; Lazarus, 1999). For Ellis, this cognitive mediation operates through our appraisals (or inferences) of events and of course via our beliefs about events, ourselves, others, and the world. That is, Ellis progresses the Stoic idea that it is how we think about events that shapes our well-being.

While the sentiment of Stoicism is somewhat captured by REBT (Robertson & Codd, 2019), the theory of REBT is not a linear translation of Stoicism. Ellis did not consider himself to be a "Stoic" (Ellis, 1994), and he made clear that REBT does not subscribe to many Stoic ideas (Ellis, 1979). We know a lot more about emotions and emotion regulation than the Stoics could have known, so REBT very much has its roots in Stoicism but is not Stoicism as such. In my view, in REBT Ellis adopts key Stoic ideas, brings them into the modern age, adapts these ideas and adds to them to create a therapeutic system that goes beyond a school of philosophy. REBT has taken elements of Stoicism, and other schools of philosophy (e.g., Taoism and Buddhism; Ellis, 1962), that speak to psychological well-being. Specifically, Stoic Ethics and Logic and their requisite practical elaborations have a prominent place within REBT, less so the metaphysical components.

Expanding the GABCDE framework

Albert Ellis' GABCDE framework is already beautifully put together and gives us a great deal of theoretical and practical information that necessitates the application of REBT. But there are extensions to the GABCDE framework that help us to better account for nuance in human emotion and might even offer additional applied opportunities for the REBT practitioner. So, briefly, I offer a theoretical expansion to REBT.

As part of my early reading into emotion as a student, I of course came across the work of Richard Lazarus. But when I started studying REBT, I became confused that the GABCDE framework, unlike Lazarus' cognitive appraisal theory (Lazarus, 1999), did not seem to indicate *what* emotion is evinced through G, A, and B. Indeed, the reader may also have noticed that at C in REBT we distinguish between UNEs and HNEs, but specific irrational beliefs do not predict specific emotions. However, by integrating some of Lazarus' ideas with Ellis' ideas, a more elaborated picture of emotion aetiology can be formed. Here, I bring REBT and Lazarus' (1999) cognitive appraisal theory (CAT) together to enable readers to better understand and predict specific types of emotion (e.g., anxiety, anger, shame) and their UNE and HNE expressions, using the work of David et al. (2002) and my own work (e.g., Chadha et al., 2019; Turner et al., 2024) as a basis.

In Lazarus' (1999) cognitive appraisal theory (CAT; also see Lazarus & Folkman, 1984; Lazarus, 1991; Smith & Lazarus, 1993), it is proposed that emotions are the result of a transaction between the goals of the individual and the representation of environmental encounters, characterized by primary and secondary cognitive appraisal. Primary appraisals are concerned with the extent to which the encounter is relevant to one's goals (goal relevance), and whether and to what the encounter is congruent or incongruent with one's goals (goal congruence and goal incongruence). Goal relevance is fundamental to whether a transaction is viewed as relevant to one's well-being, and as such, "there is no emotion without there being a goal at stake" (Lazarus, 1999, p. 92). Goal congruence/incongruence concerns whether the conditions of a transaction facilitate or thwart what the person wants, and as such, "if conditions thwart what the person wants, a negatively toned emotion is apt to follow" (Lazarus, 1999, p. 92).

Secondary appraisals concern one's resources and options for coping with the encounter and includes problem-focussed coping potential (evaluations of one's ability to act directly on the situation to bring it in accord with one's goals), and emotion-focussed coping potential (evaluations of one's ability to psychologically adjust to the situation by altering one's interpretations, desires, or beliefs; Smith & Lazarus, 1993). Additional appraisal components of accountability (blame or credit) and future expectation are also relevant to the appraisal process and help to determine the shape and intensity of the emotion in a given situation. Lazarus (1999) also posits core relational themes that make it possible to determine the precise emotion generated from a specific constellation of appraisals. For example, anxiety is associated with the core relational theme of uncertain, existential threat (Lazarus, 1991), where primary appraisals of high goal relevance and high goal incongruence combine with secondary appraisals of low emotion-focussed coping (Smith & Lazarus, 1993). Dryden (2012a) offers a similar idea of inferential themes which closely aligns with Lazarus' ideas (Dryden suggests that Adversities can *flavour* one's emotions), helping to understand why certain Adversities (As) are associated with certain Consequences (Cs).

Irrational beliefs interact with cognitive appraisals to elicit pre-event affective states such as anxiety and negative mood (Chadha et al., 2019, 2024). For example, an actor has a career goal of winning major accolades (reflecting G in REBT). She is anticipating an audition for a major film that could lead to industry recognition. The audition is thus highly relevant to the actor's goals (reflecting goal relevance in the CAT, and A in REBT), but the actor has not auditioned for a project of this significance before, is up against other great actors, and is not sure whether she will perform well (reflecting uncertain, existential threat, and high goal incongruence in the CAT, and A in REBT). She doubts her ability to cope (low coping potential in the CAT, and A in REBT), and believes that "I want to and *therefore I must* win major accolades" and that "Failure to get a major accolade would show that *I am a complete loser*" (reflecting irrational beliefs [B] in the REBT model). Thus, she experiences unhealthy anxiety and expresses this emotion maladaptively by withdrawing effort and refusing to engage with her lines, and therefore performs below what she is usually capable of (reflecting C in REBT; see Figure 2.4). Put differently, the actor carries the G into the situation, which is appraised to be adverse (A) in the sense that she perceives the situation to be goal relevant, goal incongruent, and perceives herself to have low coping potential. This A triggers the already held and endorsed irrational beliefs (B) of demandingness and depreciation, which precipitates unhealthy anxiety (C) expressed through maladaptive behaviours.

I propose that in light of a particular goal, goal relevance and goal incongruence reflect A in the REBT model; A is "adverse" to the extent that it is perceived to be an impediment to G. If A is perceived as relevant to and incongruent with G, then the stage is set for negative emotion (C), and the individual can recruit various coping responses to change A or modulate C (e.g., Ellis, 1994). However, if A impedes G, *and* the person applies irrational beliefs to G and or the A, then UNEs at C are likely to be the result. That is, because the A is rendered highly dangerous (uncertain, existential threat) to his goals (G) by the irrational beliefs, the actor in the example is likely to experience unhealthy anxiety. Thus, the formula AxB=C becomes G-AxB=C, whereby A is seen as relevant to but an impediment to G (A is perceived to thwart G).

In essence, at A we find the seeds of emotionality, and at B (if irrational) we delineate between the *healthy or unhealthy expressions* of this emotionality. Through a greater understanding of the writings of Ellis and Lazarus, it is clear that A is a vital part of emotion per se, but B is prime suspect for emotional *turmoil*.

Situational characteristics						
My goal is to win major accolades	Major audition	Novel situation, stiff competition, uncertain performance outcome	Doubts coping ability and potential for success	"I want to and therefore I must win major accolades" "Failure to get major accolades would show that I am a complete loser"	Unhealthy anxiety	Avoids preparation, withdraws effort
Alignment with CAT and REBT						
G	A			B	C	
Personal goal	High goal relevance	High goal incongruence	Low coping potential	Irrational beliefs of demandingness and depreciation	Unhealthy negative emotion	Emotion expression (action)

Figure 2.4 An example of REBT and CAT integration

The **Interdependent** *GABCDE Framework*

> Ellis has always been clear that beliefs do not cause disturbed or constructive responses to adversity. To make this claim would be tantamount to saying that beliefs are completely separate from feelings, a stance that would violate the principle of psychological interdependence that has been present in REBT theory since its inception.
>
> -Dryden (2012b, p. 84)

One aspect that is not always fully articulated in REBT works is the interdependent and reciprocal nature of the elements that make up the GABCDE framework. In how I have presented the GABCDE framework thus far, and indeed how it is presented in much REBT literature, it appears as though perception, cognition, and emotion are separated into distinct categories. However, even in his early writings, Ellis was insistent that the elements of the GABCDE framework are *interdependent* and cannot be separated (Still, 2010). The separation of these elements is really a pragmatic approach to understanding and using the framework, rather than a literal and technically accurate portrayal of how the elements relate to each other. As Still (2010) recognizes, such separation might be necessary for training and therapeutic purposes, but at a deeper level there is interdependence between the elements of the GABCDE framework. This interdependence not only more accurately reflects how the GABCDE elements function together, but also helps us as practitioners to utilize the framework in practice, especially by offering flexibility in how each element is addressed.

In the current chapter, I make the case, or rather recapitulate Ellis' (1962, 1994) assertions, that each element of the GABCDE framework is interconnected and therefore interdependent; each element is dependent on each other element. I introduce and detail the interdependent GABCDE framework, which is a representation of the interconnected nature of each element of the GABCDE framework. The interdependence of the GABCDE framework has implications for how REBT can be practiced, particularly in light of the specific and general REBT options we have as practitioners, as highlighted in the previous chapter.

Intimate interconnections

The individual elements of the GABCDE framework are intimately interconnected only by reference to the whole. To modify, or intervene with, one aspect of the GABCDE framework is to modify, or intervene with, all aspects, such is the interdependent nature of the framework. As such, whether or not an REBT practitioner drives towards specific REBT, each element of the GABCDE framework can be subject to collateral modification in a variety of ways, with a view to helping the client. The management of emotions can be achieved in various ways aside from, and alongside, belief (B) change. It is inaccurate and reductionistic to suggest that REBT is all about disputational belief change, and this inaccuracy is confounded when we as practitioners fail to draw on the many methods, aside from cognitive change, we can use to help clients. As can be seen in the interdependent GABCDE framework, because each element is related with each other element, there are multiple points of potential intervention. You can structure interventions to address any and each element of the GABCDE framework to provide a holistic approach to applying REBT. One can alter one's goals (G), attempt to change one's inferences about an event (A), and directly alter the experience of an emotion (C). Since the inception of REBT (Ellis, 1962), and throughout its historical development (Ellis, 1994), each element of the GABCDE framework is interdependent and cannot be separated (Still, 2010); a position maintained by Dryden (1994), and the current author (Turner, 2022). The interdependent GABCDE framework draws on the idea of reciprocity too, and is reflective of what we know about how cognition and emotion can fuel one another (e.g., Bandura, 2006; Cisler & Koster, 2010; Hofmann et al., 2013; Mathews & MacLeod, 2002; Memon & Treur, 2010; Mobini & Grant, 2007; Pekrun, 2006; Wenzel, 2006).

Reciprocity

In the interdependent GABCDE framework, each element (or letter) of the framework is highly interactional, and each element affects each other element reciprocally, so that changes in one element is associated with changes in others. For example, irrational beliefs (B) are echoed in our cognitions, which are articulated through language (internally and or externally) and inform our actions (C). We rehearse these irrational beliefs and thus form habits around them. If I "can't stand" frustration, I will tend to avoid demanding circumstances and shape my behaviour in service of that avoidance (C). In turn, I will temper my goals (G), since I can't tolerate, and thus choose not to face, the demanding situations that might be requisite to meaningful goals. My goals change (G), so I am less likely to meet adversity (A) to my goals (since I no longer hold those goals). How will I ever fulfil my potential, if I cannot act towards meaningful goals? Thus, one can begin to see how irrational beliefs can influence each GABC aspect of the framework to undercut fulfilment of potential.

As can be seen in Figure 2.5, each element of the framework is joined with an interaction line to indicate interdependence.

The interconnected way in which the GABCDE framework operates, widely opens the door to broader ways of working, that not only reflect specific and general REBT, but also marry with a whole host of approaches for which REBT (and CBT per se) is the foundation, such as psychological skills training (PST; Claspell, 2010). The proposed alignment between REBT and PST is covered elsewhere (Munnick et al., 2023), but in brief, the cannon of psychological skills (Andersen, 2009) is relevant and can be applied to each element of the GABCDE framework. In REBT, we do not move from G, to A, to B, to C, to D, to E. There is no real starting place and stopping place. For example, once we have covered E, we do not down tools and smoke a cigar. Rather than a linear process, it is more accurate to consider the GABCDE framework as an iterative process and guiding schematic for helping clients to regulate emotion (and of course behaviour) with a view to making the fulfilment of potential more likely. We should look to each aspect of the GABCDE framework and make use of its interconnectedness with each other aspect, to help the client in whatever ways are most helpful for them – as is the

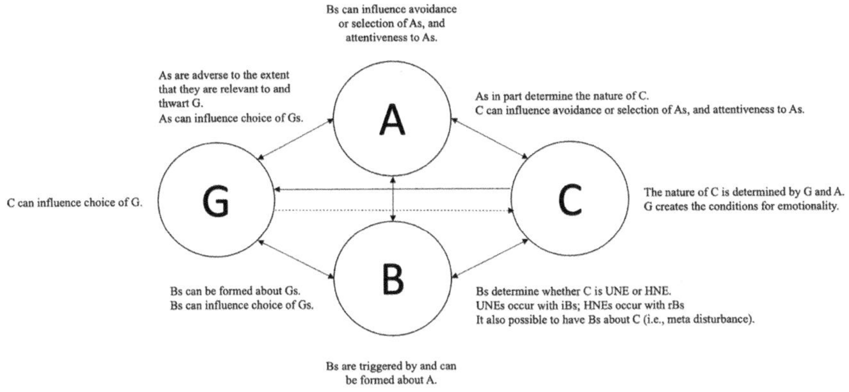

Figure 2.5 The interdependent GABCDE framework

humanistic way – remaining consistent to REBT theory and keeping the context in which we are working at the front of our minds.

Practical opportunities

In the expanded progenitor to this current book (*The Rational Practitioner*), I lavish many thousands of words on the applied implications of the interdependent GABCDE framework. But for the purposes of this primer, it is enough to understand four main things about the interdependent GABCDE in practice:

1. When one element changes, all elements change. So, when irrational beliefs are weakened as part of D, and rational beliefs are strengthened as part of E, there will be indirect implications on G, A, and C.
2. One can work with a client across all elements of the GABCDE framework. While in specific REBT we would aim to address B first, we can of course also help the client to directly address G, A, and C.
3. Especially in time limited circumstances, the REBT practitioner can legitimately help the client to directly influence any part of the GABCDE framework. Not every interaction affords the opportunity to fully dispute (D) irrational beliefs. For example, a tennis athlete experiencing anxiety five minutes prior stepping on court for a match might not be able or willing to engage in cognitive change (disputation) at B with the practitioner. In this instance, it might be more prudent to help the client practice acceptance or relaxation, image being assertive in their opening exchanges with the opening, or to positively affirm their own abilities.
4. In addressing each element of the GABCDE framework, the practitioner can use a panoply of cognitive-behavioural techniques to help the client. Theoretically consistent eclecticism is promoted, not prohibited (Dryden, 2013) and it is possible, and favourable, to approach using REBT with a pluralistic and eclectic philosophy (Neenan & Dryden, 2010).

In light of the interdependent GABCDE framework, one can focus on B specifically (i.e., specific REBT), or one can focus on G, A, and or C, as part of a holistic approach to client issues and client goal attainment (i.e., general REBT). There is no written rule that in order to apply REBT, one MUST dispute irrational beliefs and instantiate rational beliefs. This type of cognitive change characterizes *specific* REBT, but the specific and elegant solution in REBT is only one option; there are many other options. This isn't a novel edification in REBT – Ellis (1977) was quite clear that REBT can be done "elegantly" (specifically) or "inelegantly" (generally) as I have already discussed previously in the book. But why the issue about using the GABCDE framework more holistically is important within the context of interdependence, is because by focussing on A, for example, we can still instantiate changes in C – a specific focus on B is not always necessary. Of course, if assessment indicates problematic irrational beliefs, and opportunity and will is there to address these irrational beliefs, then specific REBT with an acute focus on D and E is recommended. But the practitioner can be more open to working with G, A, and C safe in the knowledge that changes in the other elements is possible (and highly probable).

A necessary complication

The reciprocity captured by the interdependent GABCDE framework adds some complication to the linear G-E narrative that is usually portrayed in REBT. However, it is a necessary and useful complication because, as I have previously mentioned, specific REBT is not the only option when working with clients. We can also use general REBT, which can have a broader focus than belief change. To be clear, in line with the primacy of cognitive change, the REBT practitioner will usually seek the elegant, specific REBT solution of belief change as a priority, but for various reasons this is not always possible or advantageous. The client may be resistant to belief change, the situation they are in might constitute an emergency or at least involve some sort of temporal limitation or restriction, or despite multiple attempts, the client is unable to comprehend the core tenets of specific REBT and thus is unlikely to engage fully in explicit belief change activities (e.g., Bowman & Turner, 2022). In these cases, the practitioner can compromise (Dryden, 1987) and execute inelegant, general, REBT (e.g., David, 2015; Dryden, 1987; Ellis, 1977), for which Dryden (2019a) presents four options, (a) change their distorted inferences, (b) change their behaviour, (c) learn new skills, and (d) change or leave the situation which provides the context for their problem.

The GABCDE framework has to be seen as dynamic because at any point in a transaction we can receive new information (from internal and external sources). Thus, each element of the framework is in constant flux, so we had better equip clients with a range of strategies that deal with each element of the GABCDE framework lest we fail to prepare them for the dynamic nature of the world they are interacting with. Indeed, in Daniel David's (2015) contemporary portrayal of REBT, practitioners can help clients to directly address A via practical problem-solving techniques (e.g., assertiveness training, conflict resolution), address C via symptomatic techniques (e.g., relaxation, meditation), without a specific focus on cognitive restructuring at B. Practitioners should keep in mind the options made available to them through both *specific* and *general* REBT modes. The main thrust of this book is specific REBT, that's for sure. But I would be lying if I said that specific REBT constituted 100% of my work with clients. By taking a holist, pluralistic, approach to REBT, we can help more people in more ways. Figure 2.6 offers the interdependent GABCDE framework without the elaboration.

Summary

It would of course have been impossible for the early Stoics to have envisioned the future importance of their ideas or the recapitulation of their philosophy within contemporary psychological theory and research. REBT in many ways flies the flag for Stoicism in this modern age, especially in its GABCDE framework. In this chapter, I introduced the GABCDE framework of REBT and cover some of its Stoic roots. What I have also tried to achieve in this chapter is to introduce the reader to the GABCDE framework of REBT, and present an alignment of Ellis' GABCDE framework and, Lazarus' CAT. The reason I have done this is to a) root REBT theory within well-supported and elaborated scientific literature, b) more fully articulate how it is that a complex constellation of cognitive processes can give rise to emotion, and c) articulate the important place that beliefs hold in emotion. I have also offered a brief explanation of the interdependent GABCDE framework. I try to make the point that it is unwise, and inaccurate, to view the GABCDE framework as sequential and or linear. It is more wise, and accurate (and helpful), to view the GABCDE framework as interactive and dynamic, whereby each element influences each other element in a synchronized and reciprocal fashion.

So, REBT is a flexible and pragmatic approach, in line with Ellis' view of REBT and in line with contemporary theory and practice, not a reductionist view of REBT

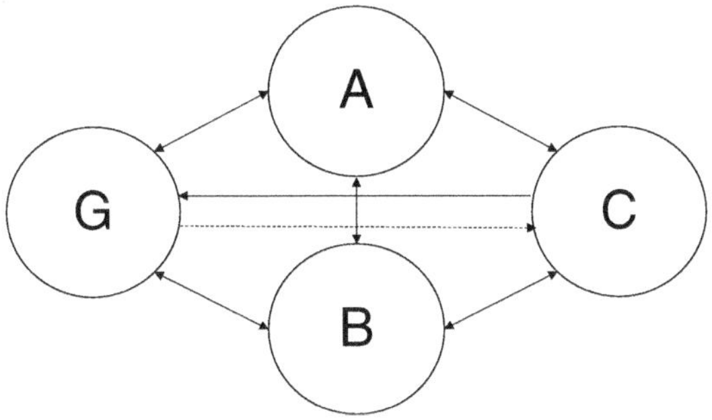

Figure 2.6 Simplified interdependent GABCDE framework

which is all about cognitive disputation and deep belief change. As Dryden and David (2008) posit,

> there can be a single approach to REBT that details belief change as its preferred target but that incorporates and targets other types of change (e.g., inferential change, behavioural change, and situational change) when belief change is not possible with certain clients or is not acceptable to others.
>
> (p. 197)

There is one REBT, and different paths to take within it (see Figure 2.7). For the purposes of the present book, to describe the path of elegant REBT (characterized by deep belief change), I use the term "specific REBT" – to describe the inelegant path of REBT (characterized by broader targets for change than only beliefs), I use the term "general REBT".

However, what I present henceforth is more reflective of *specific* REBT applied via a one-to-one mode of practice. That is, the following content focusses on the theory and application of REBT aimed towards deep philosophic change in order to make clear the distinguishing features of REBT as a framework for practice. I focus on *specific* REBT because it is clearly distinguished from other approaches, and because it represented what we might call "typical" REBT.

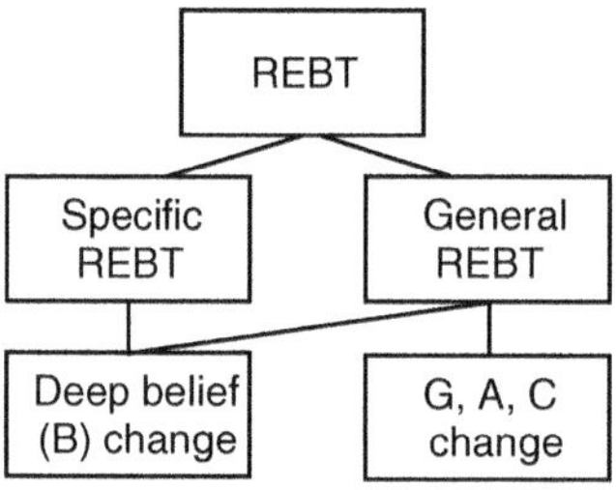

Figure 2.7 Specific REBT versus general REBT

3 Setting the foundations

The author now briefly turns to various factors that can influence the work done in REBT. I call these "foundational factors" that can facilitate or indeed hinder the work we do with clients. I also cover the main goals of REBT work and outline some typical delivery modes.

The practitioner

The nature of the practitioner-client relationship is characterized by humanistic appreciation for the client, a strong working alliance, and a collaborative goal-directed pursuit of long-term hedonism. The REBT practitioner takes a "human first, performer second" (Turner, 2016b) or a "human>performer" (Turner, 2016c) stance whereby the client is viewed as a human being, rather than viewed only in line with the vocation they pursue (e.g., actor, salesperson, athlete). As well as being factually the case, viewing the client as a human being first and foremost enables the REBT practitioner to help the person to move towards long-term (or long-range) hedonism rather than short-term hedonism. Short-term hedonism is characterized by seeking momentary pleasures only, immediate gratification (whatever the cost or danger), and striving for ease or comfort (Ellis, 1976). The REBT practitioner seeks to help the client to get better (long-term human development) rather than to feel better (short-term remediation). That is, the REBT practitioner is concerned with the long game and while vocational, relationship, and academic (for example) goals are within the purview of REBT work, these goals are superseded by the mental and physical health of the human being. To serve this long-game, the REBT practitioner teaches and encourages emotional responsibility; the notion that you can disturb, and therefore can un-disturb yourself, via your beliefs (Dryden, 2022). Ellis positioned REBT squarely as a humanistic psychotherapy (1973, 1979, 1996b), but some casual readers of REBT make the error that REBT anti-humanistic (Ellis, 1973; Finley, 1979). Ellis defined REBT as "a revolutionary humanistic approach to psychotherapy" (p. 4), and places cognitive psychotherapists (e.g., himself, Aaron T. Beck, George Kelly) alongside humanists such as Carl Rogers and Abraham Maslow. The REBT practitioner helps the client to apply what is effective, rather than what is expedient, and focusses on the person rather than the symptom (Trower & Jones, 2001).

DOI: 10.4324/9781003508472-4

The REBT practitioner challenges ideas, not people, and applies Socratic dialogue as the main discursive tool. The practitioner and the client are scientists in cahoots, applying the principles of proof, logic, and function, collaboratively (e.g., Bond, 2002) to the client's beliefs (ideas). The REBT practitioner *can be* active-directive in their work with clients in order to keep the work focussed and goal-directed, and in order to facilitate often challenging conversations. This allows the practitioner to educate the client about the GABCDE framework for example, and enables a focus on the present, rather than on the past. Psychoeducation is a hallmark of REBT, and the active-directive style allows for the use of a didactic approach to *some* elements of the work. This active-directive style is not to be read as "harsh" and "cutting" (David, 2015), and just because Albert Ellis was at times blunt in his demonstrations of REBT, the effectiveness of REBT does not rest on the practitioner's mimicry of Ellis. Importantly, the active-directive consulting style should not be applied unilaterally to all clients in all contexts and should not be adopted at the expense of the working alliance or client-practitioner rapport.

The client

REBT has been applied across a variety of ages, cross-culturally, across many contexts (Jordana et al., 2023; King et al., 2024). It is difficult to imagine for whom REBT would *not* be applicable, but if a client is not able or willing to introspect, share their thoughts, situational, emotional, and behavioural experiences, and or is resistant to conversation in general, then the REBT practitioner must work harder to form a strong connection with the client to "grease the wheels" so to speak. It is not enough to give up on a client or blame them for their disengagement. As REBT practitioners we are at pains to engage clients in as many ways as possible, given the importance of imbuing the client with the wisdom (sometimes ancient) held within REBT. It is of course possible that client reluctance is underpinned by irrational belief (e.g., "I can't stand uncomfortable conversations", "It is awful to share how I really feel"), therefore early work with a client might be concerned with helping them to express themselves and to develop strong client-practitioner rapport.

One key factor about the client that the practitioner must understand is the extent to which the client *wants* to be in the session. Does the client want to solve a problem? Or are they just looking for an ear? Figure out which it is because if the client does not want to solve their issues, REBT is not for them. REBT is not about dragging somebody unwillingly to safety, they have to partake in the process, by first expressing a desire to change. In some settings, such as with young people, it is sometimes the case that the young person has been told to, or coerced into, seeing the psychologist. In these cases, the practitioner can develop strong rapport with the client, and over a period of time start to offer some tentative advice if needed, in moments where the interaction is conducive to our input. The approach here is "since we are here together, why don't we make use of the time by having a chat?" rather than "right, I know you don't want to be here, but there is this thing called REBT".

The working alliance

When trying to ascertain the significant factors that determine the effectiveness of applied psychology (e.g., psychotherapy), the importance of the therapeutic relationship is chief and extends across the many approaches and "therapies" (e.g., Sprenkle & Blow, 2004), including CBTs (Raue & Goldfried, 1994). Regardless of theoretical orientation or client presenting issues, the development of a strong working alliance is important to the therapeutic relationship (Woody & Adessky, 2002), because it is the working alliance that makes core aspects of any approach viable. Without a client-practitioner relationship underpinned by a strong working alliance, inviable are core aspects of REBT such as setting therapeutic goals, deep excavation of thoughts and beliefs, Socratic dialogue, disputation, and adherence to therapeutic tasks. The working alliance provides the context through which counselling strategies work (e.g., Horvath & Greenberg, 1989), and as such, a good working alliance is considered to be vital for CBT success (e.g., Dobson & Shaw, 1988; Raue & Goldfried, 1994; Watson et al., 2018).

In REBT, like in other CBTs, the development and continual strengthening of a strong working alliance is important (Bernard & Dryden, 2019). There is of course recognition and application of the core conditions of empathy, unconditional acceptance, and genuineness, but while these conditions are seen as desirable, they are not seen as sufficient for therapeutic change (Dryden, 2017). The key change mechanisms and levers upon which the practitioner and client must apply pressure, are covered in detail later in this book. But I wanted to be clear here that good REBT is associated with the development and maintenance of a strong client-practitioner working alliance (Bordin, 1979). This is underpinned by a solid bond, openness, clear aims for the work, and the forthright effort expenditure towards those agreed aims (e.g., Dryden, 2009a; Dryden & David, 2008). A full guide to developing a strong working alliance is beyond the scope of the present book, but there are some illuminating guidelines elsewhere (e.g., Horvath & Greenberg, 1989). Even in REBT, where the working alliance alone is not considered sufficient to achieve change (Ellis, 2004; Dryden, 2019b), particular importance is placed on establishing and maintaining an appropriate bond with the client (Dryden et al., 2010).

The aims of the work

It is important not to assume the reasons for the client wanting to engage in the work with you. Understanding what has led the client to seeking help is important, as it can help to frame the work and ensure that the work delivers on what the client wants to get from it, so long as they have reasonable expectations for course (!). As part of developing a strong working alliance, the goals of REBT are negotiated and agreed upon by client and practitioner. It is usually for the practitioner to explain to the client what REBT is and how the work between client and practitioner might be executed. We can then address any concerns the client may have, and correct any misconceptions they have about psychology in general.

It is important that the client understands the autonomy they have in the work. The client can make use of many options during REBT – it is not a formulaic and rigid process. But what are the core aims of the work in REBT? DiGiuseppe and colleagues (2014) suggest the goals of REBT are to minimize distress, maximize the length of life, and enhance joy in the process of living (i.e., responsible hedonism). Of course, specific aims are particular to each client, and Dryden (2021) suggests developing a problem list and then figuring out what the client would rather think, feel, and do in response to adversity (A). This information then becomes the goals of the work in the short-term, with longer-term goals that are more developmental also emanating from the work. Bearing all this in mind, I propose that the broad aim of REBT work is to:

> Support the client in developing and strengthening rational ways of seeing the world in service of long-term well-being, biopsychosocial functioning, and goal fulfilment (eudaimonia).

To achieve this broad aim, there are several actions I will take:

1. I will help the client to understand that they can exert some control over their thoughts, emotions, and behaviours.
2. I will teach the client that they can re-evaluate some of the ways that they see themselves, other people, and the world. Alongside this, I will encourage the client to take a critical, scientific, stance with matters of the mind.
3. I will enable the client to develop beliefs that meet stringent criteria of truth, logic, and function.
4. I will do all of the above by interacting with the client openly and forthrightly, teaching them skills and ideas that contribute to, rather than detract from, their life.
5. The client will be actively involved in the work, not just as a passive participant, but as an active collaborator in every aspect. The client does the work – the practitioner supports the client in their undertaking.
6. I will make myself redundant. After the work has ceased, the client should go out into the world able to apply REBT independently, and we encourage the client to become their own therapist (Dryden et al., 2010).

The REBT "process"

The GABCDE framework is not to be followed in a linear or mechanical way. REBT is structured, logical, educational, directive, present-centred, future oriented, and skills focussed (e.g., Dryden, 2021). REBT is not inflexible, because we tailor the content and delivery to the client. We are not machines, but a framework is useful and helps to ensure accurate REBT. I will use the ordering of the chapters in this book to communicate the main tasks of REBT, but in brief, the tasks are:

1. Develop and strengthen the working alliance.
2. Establish the aims of the work, agree on a target problem, and a way forward.
3. Assess C – establish the existence of UNEs and HNEs concerning the target problem.
4. Assess A – establish the inference/s concerning the target problem that is/are triggering irrational beliefs (B).
5. Assess G – establish how and to what extent A impedes G in the target problem. Also, support and encourage eudaimonic goals.
6. Teach the B-C connection – educate the client in the idea of cognitive mediation.
7. Assess B – establish the existence and nature of irrational beliefs (iB) and rational beliefs (rB).
8. Teach the client about iBs and rBs, and how to distinguish between them.
9. Ensure client is able to see the connection between their Gs, As, Bs, and Cs.
10. Disputation (D) – challenge and weaken irrational beliefs.
11. Effective New Belief (E) – develop, challenge, strengthen, and commit to rational beliefs.
12. Ensure redundancy – client becomes their own "practitioner".

It is important to note that the 1–12 tasks are not necessarily in order of completion. For example, task 1 is something that is constantly refined, task 2 is often revisited, and we are continuously assessing Gs, As, Bs, and Cs with the client (tasks 3, 4, 5, and 7). So, it is hoped that the reader does not view these 12 tasks as an order of events. As an idea of the structure, in Figure 3.1, I have included a completed GABCDE assessment sheet. This sheet doubles up as a record of the main outcomes for each task of REBT with a particular client. I worked with an elite skeet shooter who was having some trouble performing to his potential when competing at larger, more prestigious, events. The client arrived with this issue, and so the direction of the work was quite clear early on. Of course, some clients will not arrive with a clear issue, but the example is illustrative rather than prescriptive. I do not provide this example to demonstrate perfect REBT (if such a thing even exists) but to illustrate the GABCDE with a real client.

Homework

It is commonly recognized that REBT is more effective when clients are engaging in some meaningful between-session activities germane to the work being undertaken (Kazantzis et al., 2010). Homework is relevant all the way through the REBT process. That is, for each of the 12 tasks I highlight above, a homework task can be negotiated to further the work in the client's own time. I would generally not use the term "homework" with the clients I work with due to its connotations with school (nobody wants to be reminded of school, surely!). The reader can call it what they like in keeping with the context they are working within, but I tend to call it "between-session training" and help the client to undertake "mental training activities" or "mental training tasks" (Turner & Barker, 2014). The homework is

C – *unwanted and unpleasant thoughts, emotions, and behaviours*
Think: distracted, mind wandering, overthinking, competitors will beat me. **Feel:** anxiety, shaking, weak, uncomfortable, poor control of body, sweating. **Behave:** fidgety, felt and acted differently to normal, isolated myself, underperformed, skill breakdown.

What thoughts, emotions, and behaviours would be more desirable?
Think: focussed, clear-minded, things just clicking, auto-polit, confident. **Feel:** nervous but relaxed, ready, strong and prepared. **Behave:** chatting, interacting with people, fluid skills, perform to, or close to, potential.

A – *in what situation did you feel the negative emotions and behaviours*
I had a major event that was very a prestigious competition. There were elite opponents, and also international scouts were watching. This was a great chance to show how good I am to the scouts, so underperformance here would ruin my changes.

G – *your career and life goals*
To be the best I can be in my sport To be content with my contribution to the world

How is A stopping you from attaining G?
If I don't perform well at this event, then it might ruin my selection chances. If I underperform at events like this, then I will not be able to reach my potential.

B – *your beliefs about A that led to C*
1. "If I underperform, I'm a loser, failure, worthless". 2. "I want to be, and so I must be, thought of as one of the best, or else I'm nothing". 3. "I can't stand failing when it matters".

D – *Disputing your* **irrational B's**
Evidence Q: Where is the evidence for these beliefs? Are they true? **A: There is no evidence. No rules, nothing written at all. I know I can stand failing because I have come back from defeat many times. It is not true that failing makes me a loser – failing just means I have failed, that's it.**

Logic

Q: Are these beliefs logical?
A: No, they are not. They are not consistent with reality. Just because I want something, does not mean I must have it. The world doesn't owe me anything.

Helpfulness

Q: Are these beliefs helping your performance? Are these beliefs moving you towards your goals?
A: No – they are actually harming my performance and reducing my chances of reaching my goals.

E – *Replacing your irrational B's with rational B's*
1. "If I underperform, I'm a loser, failure, worthless"
If I underperform, it does not mean I am a loser, it just means I failed, which I am allowed to do as a human being.
2. "I want to be, and so I must be, thought of as one of the best, or else I'm nothing"
I would like to be, but I don't have to be, thought of as one of the best. If this doesn't happen though, I can accept myself and am certainly not 'nothing'
3. "I can't stand underperforming when it matters"
Failing is really tough, but I can stand it. Although I don't like it, underperforming will not end me, and it is worth tolerating it so I can learn and improve.

Figure 3.1 Example GABCDE assessment sheet from the author's work with a skeet shooter

to be negotiated between client and practitioner, not "set" by the practitioner. This is so that the client takes ownership over the work, feels capable of completing the work (with some effort), and so that they see a clear purpose in the work (Dryden, 2019c). Sufficient time should be spent negotiating the specifics of the task (when will they do it and how?) and this element of the session is not to be tagged onto the end of a session when time is running out. We want the client to actually complete the task, so it makes no sense to negotiate an activity that is too difficult or stressful for them to complete. Also, it is vital to review homework completion in each session as a meaningful part of the session. This can bring meaning to the homework and to ensure proper reflection. Clients that do not complete homework should not be admonished – rather – we need to get to the bottom of *why* they failed to complete the task. Their avoidance of the task might indicate some faulty inference and or irrational beliefs about the task that can be addressed in session. Also, perhaps we did not set the right task.

Homework tasks tend to fit into three main categories of cognitive, emotive, and behavioural, and we would try to include all categories of homework in our work. Cognitive activities could include the client reading some relevant material, listening to podcasts, or engaging in psychoeducational content. Tasks could also include noting down their Gs, As, Bs, and Cs in the early parts of the work (on a blank version of Figure 3.1), and practicing D and E in mid to latter parts. They could use the Smarter Thinking App (Turner & Wood, 2019a) for example. Also, I tend to use psychometrics as cognitive assignments too. I would use the Smarter Thinking Profile (Turner & Wood, 2019b) or the irrational performance beliefs inventory (Turner et al., 2018b) to measure irrational beliefs, and use specific questionnaires that monitor emotional and behavioural issues germane to the client's issue/s. Emotive tasks could include imagery in which the client might picture themselves in their minds eye facing A and practicing a healthy response (via rational belief usage). Behavioural tasks could include risk-taking exercises, which involves the client forthrightly facing the A that they fear and or have been avoiding. This can show that the A is not unbearable or awful, for example. A client with disapproval irrational beliefs ("I cannot bear being disapproved of") could assertively speak up in a team meeting at work, for example. An athlete afraid of failure, with failure irrational beliefs ("I must not fail and failure is awful"), could or try new things in training – force the failure in order to realize that it is not fatal! Behavioural exercisers are not just about facing A, they could include practicing relaxation, for example.

A "typical" session

There is of course no real "typical" REBT session because the work we do with clients is idiosyncratically tailored to each client. But, REBT does have a structure and there are guidelines we can apply to the flow of a session in order to ensure we stay on task with the work we are doing. We cannot, or should not, just meander our way through REBT sessions with no structure or purpose. Below, I have adapted DiGiuseppe et al.'s (2014) session outline for a 50-minute session that can be used as a guide:

First 10 minutes

- Ice-breaker/rapport building (yes, in every session).
- Old business from the previous session.
- New business: any major life changes.
- Check on homework.
- Setting the agenda for the session.

Middle 30 minutes

- Work time, in which the aims of the work are pursued.

Last 10 minutes

- Summary of work done in the session.
- Negotiation of homework and identification of barriers to completion.
- Closing questions.

In my experience, we do not usually get 45–60 minutes and often one-to-one sessions are ad hoc, unplanned, sprung upon us. We have to be flexible with the way we use REBT because we are not always going to get the structure and time needed for a "typical" session as outlined above. Luckily, REBT can be applied very briefly, and effective sessions (or conversations) can be achieved in as little as 15 minutes (see Dryden, 2018). So, imagine crunching the "typical" session down to 15 minutes, what elements would remain? For me, it looks like this:

First 3 minutes

- Ice-breaker/rapport building (e.g., "How have things been?" "How was training earlier?" "Did you see the game last night?").
- Setting the agenda for the session (e.g., "What do you want to talk about today?" "What can we get done?" "What shall we do with our time?").

Middle 10 minutes

- Work time, in which the aims of the work are pursued.

Last 2 minutes

- Summary of work done in the session ("To wrap things up . . ." "so, going forward you say you are going to . . ." "so let's try x today/over the next week/in your next training session, and see how things go".
- Closing questions (e.g., "is there anything else you wanted to talk to me about?" "Do you have any questions about what we talked about today?").

Notice that formal homework setting does not appear here, and this is because often these ad hoc sessions do not happen in the context of consistent and ongoing work with the client, and may be the first and last time we see the client (e.g., Dryden, 2016). We have to be realistic about what is achievable in very brief sessions, but ultimately, we are trying to help the client to solve an issue or problem, or we are helping them develop in some way or other, so we can a) be very targeted in our work, b) be guided by what the client wants, and c) make use of the interdependent GABCDE framework. While we can still be very Socratic in our interaction with the client, a more direct approach is often needed to make the most of the short time and give the client something to work with and apply. We have to be pragmatic and help as much as we can within the contextual constraints we are faced with, if we are to work effectively in congruence with the context that the client operates within or inhabits.

How about a 5-minute session? What elements would remain? For me, it tends to look like this:

First 1 minute

- Setting the agenda for the session (e.g., "What do you want to talk about today?" "What can we get done?" "What shall we do with our time?").

Middle 4 minutes

- Work time, in which the aims of the work are pursued.

Last 1 minute

- Summary of work done in the session ("To wrap things up . . ." "so, going forward you are going to . . ." "so let's try x today/over the next week/in your next training session, and see how things go").

No time for ice breaking, no time for closing questions here. We cut to the chase and prioritize forming a solution to a very well-defined issue. These interactions typically take place on the phone when clients call for a brief chat amidst their daily activities. In the sport setting, which I am very familiar with, this might also be a face to face conversation in a competition venue prior to a game, walking with an athlete between training sessions, encounters court/pitch side before/during/after training, on the bus on the way to training/competitions, at dinner cuing up for food (!). You may need to sacrifice some Socratic dialogue here and offer some things for the client to try based on your reading of the issue. But again, there is little need to stray from the GABCDE framework.

A "typical" REBT programme

In the previous section, we asked "is there a 'typical' session?" and here we ask "is there a 'typical' programme?" In light of the flexible way that we often have to work, we may never actually formulate a programme of work with a client. Some clients interact with the practitioner transiently and therefore the formal articulation of a programme may not be possible, relevant, or needed. But when working outside the confines of an organization (i.e., private work with one client), there is a greater capacity to develop and follow a programme of work, because we can be more planned with the time we have and we are more likely to get dedicated and sufficient time with the client in which to implement said programme.

We know that a full REBT programme is guided by the 12 tasks are highlighted earlier in the chapter. But how many sessions should we use to complete these tasks? Research indicates anywhere between a single session (Bowman & Turner,

2022) to 8 sessions (Wood et al., 2020) of between 20 minutes to 60 minutes length for each session, can be effective (Jordana et al., 2023). But as indicated previously, I would often have 5- and 15-minute sessions with clients. For private clients with whom I have more autonomy over the work, I would plan for 10 sessions as the best-case scenario and if we have *properly* completed our work in less than 10 sessions, then great! The flow of the sessions is dictated in part by the aforementioned 12 tasks but really is determined by the client. That is, the specifics of the work are dictated by the nature of the issues, the goals of the client, and the progress the client makes. But having a plan means at least we are not going into the work blind to the possible direction and flow of the work. Realistically, the plan will change because people, situations, emotions, change. So again, be flexible and do not just stick to the plan for the sake of it and sacrifice the ability to be sensitive and reactive to a changing context. The contexts we are working in are often uncontrollable, ever changing, and unpredictable. We cannot compensate for these contextual challenges by being rigid in our approach to work, but we can at least initially offer a plan to the client to provide some much-needed structure, and we can attempt to stay on track, flexibly making changes if needed.

Summary

In this chapter, I have covered the major client, practitioner, and logistic considerations when applying REBT. What I stress here in particular is the development and fostering of a strong working alliance, some procedural consistency in applying REBT regardless of context or mode, and practitioner flexibility. While I offer some guidance on programme and session structure, flow, and content, this is all dependent on the client, their issues and goals, and the context in which we are working. Regardless of the specifics of the work, we can comfortably apply the GABCDE framework of REBT.

Next, I move onto the specific procedural components of REBT. I structure the remaining chapters using the order by which I would *typically* work *through* the GABCDE framework, and is geared to towards specific REBT. In what follows, I present each element of the framework in the order in which the element is *typically* addressed in my REBT practice. Therefore, I first cover C, then A, then G, followed by B, before moving onto D and E. Regardless of the precise ordering, GABC should be fully assessed before moving to D and E, and for the purposes of this book, I believe the reader is furnished with sufficient detail for each element to be able to reorder the process as the situation determines.

4 Consequences (C): Emotional, behavioural, cognitive

What have you come to see me about? What seems to be troubling you at the moment? What can I help you with today? Perhaps you could tell me what has brought you to see me?

All of the above questions are formulated to elicit from the client the first pieces of information that will help the practitioner to get some insight into the nature of the client's issues. Quite often, the answers to these questions contain emotional material. Often, the reason prospective clients approach me to undertake some psychology support, is because they are experiencing, or have experienced, an unwanted and unpleasant emotion. This emotion is usually associated with, or perceived to be, a hindrance to goal attainment and or well-being by the client. As such, they wish to ameliorate the emotion and its behavioural concomitants which are often life limiting. They wish to do this in part because the emotion is unpleasant and unwanted – in other words, they are suffering and are motivated to ameliorate this suffering now and avoid this suffering in the future. But they also wish to do this because the emotion is limiting their ability to fulfil their potential.

Healthy versus unhealthy negative emotions

The core work undertaken here for the client and practitioner, is to determine whether the emotions being experienced are unhealthy negative emotions (UNEs) or healthy negative emotions (HNEs). Although a client may be experiencing a negatively valenced, and thus often unpleasant, emotion, does not mean that this emotion is a hindrance to their well-being or goal attainment. In REBT, the aim is not to help clients remove negative emotion completely – we do not believe that this would be advantageous – not all "negative" emotions are disturbed or appropriate targets for change (DiGiuseppe et al., 2014). As Kashdan and Biswas-Diener (2014) point out, negative emotion can be very useful (functional) as sources of information concerning our progress, interactions, environment, and actions. REBT theory does not imply that negative emotions are *desirable* but holds that they are an essential part of both adaptation and coping in the face of activating events (Turner et al., 2018a, 2019a). It is not the mere experience of negative emotion that is problematic, but how intense, pervasive, and ultimately, disruptive the emotion is.

DOI: 10.4324/9781003508472-5

In REBT emotions are targets for change when they are unhealthy (UNEs), not when they are negative. It is the function of the emotion that is important in REBT, not the valence. UNEs are justifiable targets for change within REBT. HNEs are associated with adaptive behaviours or action tendencies (actual and or intended) and healthy physiological responses, whereas UNEs are associated with maladaptive behaviours or action tendencies (actual and or intended) and unhealthy physiological responses (e.g., David & Cramer, 2010). The distinction between HNEs and UNEs concerns function, adaptiveness, appropriateness, and health. HNEs are functional, adaptive, appropriate, and healthy, while UNEs are dysfunctional, maladaptive, inappropriate, and unhealthy. HNEs are self-enhancing, while UNEs are self-defeating. HNEs lead to constructive behaviour and aid goal attainment, while UNEs lead to unconstructive behaviour and interfere with goal attainment (Dryden, 2021). The concepts of HNEs and UNEs are captured in the REBT-derived Binary Theory of Emotional Distress (BTED; Ellis & DiGiuseppe, 1993). For a critical discussion see Turner et al. (2018a, 2019a), and detailed description of UNEs and HNEs can be seen in Figure 4.1.

In practice as REBT practitioners, the question we must ask when determining the UNE or HNE status of an emotion is:

> *Is the emotion functional, adaptive, and appropriate for the attainment of long-term eudaimonia?*

It is not that the client *must* present with a UNE in order for the practitioner to apply REBT. As I have previously stated in this book, using the GABCDE holistically we can apply REBT with clients who wish to down-regulate (or indeed up-regulate) an emotion, even if the emotion does not qualify as a UNE. Thus, even if the client presents with healthy anxiety, they may still wish to exercise more control over the anxiety, and can thus apply various emotion regulation strategies covered previously in the present book and in other works (Turner, 2022). We can help the client to express the emotion in as functional way as possible, help them to quell the emotion, and we can help them to weaken irrational beliefs and strengthen rational beliefs. But most importantly, we can educate the client in the idea that negative emotions per se are not the enemy of performance and well-being.

One of the ways we can help the client to understand the functionality or dysfunctionality of C, and motivate them towards working against the UNE and towards the HNE is to foster some cognitive dissonance. We can ask the client to think about an area of their life in which they experience and express HNEs, and to compare that functional experience with the dysfunctional experience they are reporting in relation to their main issue. The idea that they do experience HNEs, and therefore can move towards these HNEs in this instance (and in any instance) can help the client to realize that their current way of being is not serving them and can strengthen their will to change – to bring about HNEs and ameliorate UNEs.

G-A		*B*	*C*		
Appraisal	*Core Relational Theme*	*Belief*	*Healthy or Unhealthy*	*Example Cognitive Consequences*[*]	*Example Action Tendencies (actual or intended)*[*]
High Goal Relevance High Goal Incongruence Low/uncertain (emotion-focussed) coping potential	Threat/Danger Facing uncertainty and existential threat	Irrational	Unhealthy Anxiety	• Overestimate probability and or magnitude of threat. • Has more task-irrelevant thoughts.	• Withdraw physically and or mentally from the threat (avoidance). • Ward off the threat (e.g., superstitious behaviour). • Seek reassurance and or protection. • Perform below potential. • Tranquilize feelings. • Over preparation. • Risk aversion. • Hide or distract self from threat. • Keep checking on status of threat. • Hypervigilance to threat.
		Rational	Healthy Anxiety	• Realistic about the probability and or magnitude of threat. • More task relevant thoughts.	• Face up to threat (approach). • Deal with the threat constructively. • Take constructive action to reduce/minimize the risk or danger. • Perform to potential. • Appropriate preparation. • Take calculated risks. • Seek support to help self to face threat. • Appropriate awareness of threat.

High Goal Relevance High Goal Incongruence Low (problem-focussed) coping potential Low/negative future-expectancy	Irrevocable loss or failure (with implications for the future) Helplessness about harm or loss Undeserved plight	Irrational	Unhealthy Sadness (non-clinical depression)	• See only negative aspects of the loss or failure. • Think of other losses and failures that one has experienced. • Think one is unable to self-help (helplessness) • Hopelessness.	• Withdraw into oneself. • Create an environment consistent with feelings. • Attempt to terminate feelings in self-destructive ways. • Over-dependence on others. • Push people away. • Bemoan one's fate.
		Rational	Healthy Sadness	• Able to recognize both negative and positive aspects of the loss or failure. • Able to self-help. • Able to look to the future with hope.	• Express feelings about the loss or failure (e.g., talk about these to significant others). • Seek out reinforcements after a period of mourning. • Allow self to be comforted. • Create environment inconsistent with feelings.
High Goal Relevance High Goal Incongruence Other/world-accountability Self-accountability	Self- or other-blame for goal obstruction, threat to self-esteem, or transgression of personal rule A demeaning offense against me and mine Frustration Other shames or ridicules me	Irrational	Unhealthy Anger	• Overestimate the extent to which the other person acted deliberately. • See malicious intent in the motives of others. • See self as definitely right; other(s) seen as definitely wrong. • Unable to see the other person's point of view. • Plot revenge.	• Attack the self/other physically. • Attack the self/other verbally. • Attack the self/other passive-aggressively. • Displace attack onto another person, animal or object. • Alienate others. • Withdraw aggressively. • Recruit allies against perceived transgressor.

G-A		B	C		
		Rational	Healthy Anger	• Do not overestimate the extent to which the other person acted deliberately. • Do not see malicious intent in the motives of the other(s). • Do not see self as definitely right and the other(s) as definitely wrong. • Able to see the other's point of view. • Do not plot revenge.	• Assert self with the other. • Request, but not demand, behavioural change from the other. • Non-aggressively step-away from an unsatisfactory situation after attempting to deal with it.
High Goal Relevance High Goal Incongruence Self-accountability	Hurt the feelings of significant others Having transgressed a moral imperative, code, or rule (i.e., act immorally, unethically) Self-blame	Irrational	Unhealthy Guilt	• Assume that one has definitely committed the sin. • Assume more personal responsibility than is warranted. • Assign less responsibility to others than is warranted. • Do not put behaviour into overall context. • Think that one deserves and will get retribution.	• Look for ways to escape from the guilt in self- defeating ways. • Beg forgiveness from the person wronged and or reject offers of forgiveness. • Promise unrealistically that they will not "sin" again. • Disclaim responsibility for wrongdoing. • Punish self physically or by depreciation. • Make excuses for behaviour.

		Rational	Healthy Guilt	• Consider behaviour in context when making judgements concerning the "sin". • Assume appropriate level of personal responsibility to self and others. • Take into account mitigating factors. • Put behaviour into overall context. • Do not think they deserve or will get retribution.	• Face up to the healthy pain that accompanies the sin. • Ask, but not beg, for forgiveness. • Understand reasons for wrongdoing. • Atone for the sin by taking a penalty. • Make appropriate amends. • No tendency to make excuses for one's behaviour or display defensive behaviour. • Accept offers of forgiveness.
High Goal Relevance High Goal Incongruence Self-accountability	Being looked down on by others (i.e., others' negative judgement) Having failed to live up to (i.e., falling short of) an ego-ideal Actions reflected badly on social ingroup	Irrational	Unhealthy Shame	• Overestimate the "shamefulness" of the information revealed. • Overestimate the likelihood that the judging group will notice or be interested in the information. • Overestimate the degree of disapproval self (or reference group) will receive. • Overestimate the length of time any disapproval will last.	• Remove self from the "gaze" of others. • Isolate self from others. • Save face by attacking other(s) who have "shamed" self. • Defend threatened self-esteem. • Ignore attempts by others to help.

G-A		*B*	*C*		
		Rational	Healthy Shame	• Sees information revealed in a compassionate self-accepting way. • Is realistic about the likelihood that the judging group will notice or be interested in the information. • Is realistic about the degree of disapproval. • Is realistic about the length of time the disapproval will last.	• Continue to participate actively in social interaction. • Respond to attempts of others to restore social equilibrium.

Figure 4.1 The articulated GABC framework incorporating Ellisian and Lazarusian concepts

Source: In part adapted from David et al., 2002, 2005; Dryden, 2012a, 2018; Dryden & Branch, 2008; Smith & Lazarus, 1993

*Examples are not exhaustive, in part, because people are idiosyncratic in their C expression, and thus these examples are rules of thumb, not gospel.

Assessing C

Whether or not C is a HNE or UNE can be ascertained by carefully clarifying whether the emotion helps or hinders the client's goal attainment and or long-term health and well-being. The practitioner is being steered here by what the client reports in terms of how the emotion is limiting or detracting from a contented or fulfilled life. The practitioner is assessing the healthiness (HNE versus UNE) of the client's emotions by gaining information on the cognitive, physiologic (somatic), and behavioural (actual or overt, intention or impulse) aspects of the emotion. The behavioural components of the emotion are perhaps most important because they illustrate how the emotion is expressed, which can have clear implications on how the client engages with their environment. So, to identify whether the client is experiencing a UNE or a HNE, we need to assess their reported concomitant behaviours (overt) or action tendencies (impulses, intentions) when they are experiencing the emotion (Dryden, 2012a). The extent to which UNEs are dysfunctional, and HNEs are functional, is determined largely by the intended or actual expression of maladaptive or adaptive behaviours.

- UNEs involve maladaptive (destructive, self-defeating) behaviours that do not enable the client to modify or adapt to As, or successfully pursue Gs.
- HNEs involve adaptive (constructive, self-enhancing) behaviours that do enable the client to modify or adapt to As, and successfully pursue Gs (Dryden & Branch, 2008).

In other words, is the emotion and its associated cognitive, physiologic (somatic), and behavioural components, *appropriate* (HNE) or inappropriate (UNE) for the pursuit of goal attainment, fulfilment, eudaimonia? In assessing C, it is important to distinguish between overt behaviours and action tendencies. Action tendencies reflect impulses to act in a certain manner, which could be suppressed by the client, so the behaviour is not enacted (Dryden, 2012a). The reader could consider action tendencies to be behavioural *intentions* aligned with the emotion. There might be contextual restrictions that do not permit a client to literally avoid an anxiety provoking situation, but all the same, they *want* to avoid the situation and believe that only by avoiding the situation can they control their anxiety. This would be evidence of a UNE (e.g., unhealthy anxiety) because it is evidence of an *intention* to avoid (they would avoid, if they could). The client may not always act in a way that aligns with their UNE (Dryden & Branch, 2008).

We can undertake C assessment by developing a conversation with the client concerning the specific details of their emotional experience. The practitioner asks a variety of open questions in order to understand what the client was thinking, doing (or intending to do), and feeling, when they were experiencing the emotion, or when in the specific situation. When doing this, it is important to avoid questions that reinforce or suggest an A-C connection (Dryden & Branch, 2008). That is, the REBT practitioner avoids questions such as, "how did that make you feel?", "did that make you angry?", or "what emotion did that cause within you?". Rather, the

REBT practitioner would ask questions like, "when that happened, how did you feel?", "what feelings did you experience in that situation?", or "how did you feel *about* that?" (Dryden & Branch, 2008). This can be applied to questions pertaining to the thoughts and behaviours of the client too (e.g., "when that happened, how did you act or want/intend to act?" or "what were you thinking in that situation?").

Based on the client's responses, the practitioner and the client can start to determine the precise emotion in question, and whether what they were thinking, doing, and feeling are healthy (i.e., in service of the client's goals and well-being), or unhealthy (i.e., counter to the client's goals and well-being). For example, if a client responds to the question "when that happened, how did you feel?" with the answer "down", then we do not know precisely what they are experiencing, and have no details about the cognitive or behavioural aspects of this feeling. So, we need to dig a bit deeper here in order to clarify the client's emotion, and then whether the emotion is a UNE or HNE. Encourage the client to report what they *feel* or what *emotion* they experienced, because clients can often be vague or report inferences, rather than emotions. Just be patient and if needed, explain to the client the differences between thoughts and emotions in order to help them supply the information you seek.

As a way to orient the particular methods of client questioning around C, we can ask the client to recall a recent and concrete situation in which the emotion was experienced so that they can better detail how they felt, thought, and behaved (or wanted to behave). If a recent event is not apparent, then the client can use a particularly powerful memory they have of the emotion being experienced, or they can give an account of how the emotion typically plays out in relevant situations. From my experience, the more recent and concrete, the better, because detail is paramount. We can ask the client directly about what is going wrong for them currently, and if things were going right, how it would look and feel. In other words, we can help them to lay out the ways in which their current C is hindering goal attainment and the ways in which an alternate C might aid their goal attainment. Once we have painted a realistic (not utopic) picture of how they would like to function (think, feel, behave), we can help animate the client towards realizing that picture. We can do this Socratically by having the client conceptualize a C that would best help them, or we can provide some potential alternate Cs to help the client conceptualize healthy negative emotion. For example, a client who is unhealthy anxious about an upcoming selection trial can be Socratically encouraged to formulate a more functional C (e.g., "how would you like to think, feel, and behave when approaching this event?"), or they can be directed towards healthy anxiety (e.g., "perhaps it is possible feel anxious, but in a helpful way?"). Either way, we are communicating to the client that there is a different way to think, feel, and behave that might serve them, rather than hamper them.

Flavour of emotion

The adaptive and maladaptive cognitive and behavioural concomitants of various UNEs and HNEs can be found in Figure 4.1. This can help practitioners to assess the presence of UNEs and HNEs in what the client is experiencing. By thoroughly and accurately assessing C, we can also begin to understand the precise nature of A, following Lazarus' (1999) core relational themes. For example, if the assessment shows that the client is experiencing unhealthy anger, then following Smith and Lazarus' (1993) taxonomy for anger, we can surmise that the client may have perceived "a demeaning offence against me and mine" and may have appraised high goal relevance, low goal congruence, and high self or other-accountability (self or other-blame). A determine the "flavour of an emotion" (Dryden, 2012a, p. 7), while the rational/irrational beliefs determine whether the emotion is expressed as a UNE or an HNE. Whether and to what extent this anger is unhealthy or healthy must be determined by the practitioner, based on an assessment of the specific characteristics of the emotion, in terms of behavioural and cognitive expression.

A HNE example: upfront and honest

SP: So, when your boss told you that you were underperforming, what feelings did you experience?

Chris: I got angry.

SP: Angry?

Chris: Yes, very.

SP: And tell me Chris, when experiencing this anger, were there any actions that went along with this?

Chris: No not really. I just came away from the situation because my colleagues were present.

SP: Well, if you could have done something, if your colleagues were not present, what would you have done?

Chris: I would have told him that I don't agree with him, but that he is entitled to his opinion. But I don't agree with him!

SP: OK, how would approach this?

Chris: I would just be upfront and honest, not aggressive or anything. Just stern, and sure.

In the above example, the client indicates an appropriate intention to act in an assertive way here, and thus, it would appear that the anger experienced by the client is healthy (HNE). It is understandable that the client would be angry – they feel that they have been transgressed in a way that obstructs their goals. But the client is able to incorporate useful and appropriate behavioural intentions.

A UNE example: aggressive and violent

SP: So, when your boss told you that you were underperforming, what feelings did you experience?

Chris: I got angry.

SP: Angry?

Chris: Yes, very.

SP: And tell me Chris, when experiencing this anger, were there any actions that went along with this?

Chris: I ran up to him and went to grab him. My colleagues had to pull me away from the situation to be honest.

SP: I see. If they had not pulled you away, what would you have done?

Chris: I would have told him that he's an idiot and that he doesn't know what he is talking about. There is no way I am underperforming.

SP: OK, anything else?

Chris: I'd have probably punched him to be honest. I was this close (client gestures with thumb and forefinger) to hitting him.

SP: So things would have got physical?

Chris: Yes. I can't let him get away with this, and to hell with colleagues who disagree with me.

In the above example, the client indicates an inappropriate intention to act in an aggressive and violent way, and thus, it would appear that the anger experienced by the client is unhealthy (UNE). So, while the client's anger is understandable, the client is wanting and attempting to incorporate destructive and inappropriate behavioural intentions. As such, our work here would be to steadfastly attenuate this UNE (unhealthy anger) via REBT, and move towards HNE (healthy anger). The issue here is not whether or not the client should be angry, but rather, the extent to which the anger is healthy or unhealthy.

Summary

In this chapter I discussed the C element of the GABCDE framework. I distinguished between HNEs and UNEs and explained some of the main ways a practitioner can assess C. The assessment of C involves exploring the emotion in detail with the client and taking a largely person-centred approach to the conversation. The job here is to non-judgmentally help the client to communicate the nature of the emotional experience as accurately as possible in as many ways as it takes for you to grasp whether a UNE or HNE is being experienced. If the details are not forthcoming, then the practitioner can move to the assessment of A, instead (for the time being!) which can often help to bring C information to light.

5 Adversity or activating event (A)

In REBT, people have goals (G) and at times (inevitably) unfortunate and undesirable occurrences, known as adversities or activating events (A), interfere with the attainment of these goals (Ellis, 1994; Shea, 2016). Importantly, trials are not only the norm, but can actually be advantageous for human development and fulfilment. It is in this spirit of acknowledgement and acceptance that we approach As in REBT. As has been posited in this book, G and A are related; A is adverse to the extent that it is relevant to and represents an impediment to (or is incongruent with) G. An integrative approach to emotion views emotions as reactions to action outcomes in relation to an individual's goals (Carver & Scheier, 1998), and the goal construct is invoked both as reason to act and as leading to emotions when obstructed or facilitated (Frijda, 1986; Kreibig et al., 2010).

Pursuing meaningful Gs can bring about positive emotions if we receive feedback that we are making positive progress towards the goal. But meaningful Gs can also bring about negative emotions because you are limited and fallible as human beings, and by pursuing these goals you will undoubtedly face challenges, barriers, and setbacks – the world, and the people you engage with and contend with, are not predictable, controllable, or wholly benign. You will fail, be rejected, be treated unfairly, and suffer in pursuit of meaningful goals. Even if you achieve your meaningful goals, this attainment with set forth new challenges, new As. The mere experience of A implies G, because A is adverse to the extent that it is perceived to thwart G. For example, an A such as "I failed in an important task" implies a G of succeeding (or not failing) in the task, or implies a less proximal G for which this particular A is seen as incongruent (e.g., being seen as perfect).

What are As?

What types of adversities (As) am I referring to in this chapter and book? I could provide a full list of As for reference, but this would take up the entire book (and then some), because As are ubiquitous, copious, and unquantifiable. This is in part because As are definitionally idiosyncratic within the individual – one client's adversity may not be adverse at all to a different client, partly because people's Gs are idiosyncratic – and also in part because we can, as human beings, creatively invent our own As seemingly out of nowhere (see Mahoney, 1974, for a protracted

DOI: 10.4324/9781003508472-6

and critical discussion on symbolic self-stimulation), often out of satiated monotony. In brief, whether and to what extent a stimulus is viewed as adverse is highly variable due to the individual differences in perception and cognitive appraisal.

In short, *A is the aspect of the situation that the person focusses on and evaluates* (Dryden, 2017). Adversities (As) typically fall into the following categories: failure, rejection, disapproval, uncertainty, lack of control, betrayal, unfairness, illness, injury, frustration, and criticism. A typical A could be "not achieving what one sets out to achieve", or "not being respected by people that matter to me", or "being treated unfairly by one's peers", or "being rejected by somebody important to me". . . you get the picture. We cannot go into our work with clients assuming to know what As will be presented or revealed, and we cannot help them to deal with every A in their world. So, part of utilizing A in REBT is about boiling the many representations of A down to the most potent and salient A. We call this the "critical A".

Critical "A"

REBT practitioners attempts to uncover the critical A (Dryden, 1995, 2009a), which is the A that the client is most disturbed about and is most proximal to the irrational belief/s. This is vital because not all As activate irrational beliefs (note: in this book I use "adversity" for A, but one can also use "activating event" because the B is activated by the A), so the practitioner had better help the client to find the critical A or else the work may become tangential and fruitless, and will not address the UNE at C. It is important to understand that the A is usually inferential, reflecting a perception or an evaluation of something that has happened (or will happen), but could be completely internal (i.e., no external event has taken place). By accurately defining the critical A we can be sure that we are dealing with the root of the emotion being experienced by the client at C. If the practitioner's assessment at C reveals anger, then it is more likely that the critical A will reflect a misdemeanour against me or mine, alongside self or other-blame, for example.

But we do not need to assume the critical A on the basis of C. The REBT practitioner can use various strategies to dig a little deeper into the presenting As to understand which As are "non-critical", and which A is "critical". For example, the author most frequently uses inference chaining, which was introduced by Moore (1983), but has been refined, developed, and extended over the years (Dryden, 1995, 1989; Neenan & Dryden, 1996, 1999a). Inference chaining

> links the client's personally significant inferences about an activating event (A) in order to find the one (sometimes called the critical A) which triggers her irrational belief (B) which then, in turn, directly leads to her emotional reactions at C.
>
> (Neenan & Dryden, 1999a, pp. 95–96)

The links are created by "Let's assume" . . . "then what?" . . . "so what?" questions, starting with the UNE. A good example of inference chaining can be found in

Ellis and Dryden (1997) on page 35, but for a simplified example, a client (Kelly) presents with shame (UNE) in response to "stuttering during a work presentation" (assumed A). The psychologist (P) enquires:

P: Tell me Kelly, what is shame-provoking in your mind about stuttering in the presentation?
Kelly: Well, everybody saw me do it. It was mortifying!
P: Would you have been as ashamed if nobody saw you do it?
Kelly: No because nobody would have known! But it's more the fact that certain people saw me stutter . . .
P: Certain people?
Kelly: Well, my boss, colleagues, juniors, saw it.
P: Why would that bring about shame?
Kelly: Well, they probably judged me. They probably questioned my ability.
P: Let's assume that is the case. What if they did judge you and questioned your ability?
Kelly: It would mean that I've let them all down.
P: Ok let's assume that you have let them all down. Why is that so bad?
Kelly: They've supported me and given me opportunities, and then I go and let them all down. What a thing to do!
P: What do you mean by "what a thing to do"?
Kelly: Letting them all down like that. That's the worst thing in the world to me. It would be awful.
P: When you say "it" would be awful. What are you referring to here as being awful?
Kelly: Letting people who are important to me down.
P: So, are you ashamed of letting these people down because you think it would be awful?
Kelly: Yes. It IS awful. For me, there is nothing worse in life.

In the above, it is possible to see how the non-critical A of missing on open goal is not challenged for its validity. Rather, it is assumed to be true so that we can dig a little deeper to uncover the critical A (Neenan & Dryden, 1996), which is the prospect of letting significant others down. This closely ties to the irrational beliefs of awfulizing ("It would be awful to let people down"), which we would take further into the assessment of B to instantiate a full irrational belief (primary and secondary) derived from a preference (e.g., "I want to and therefore I must have the approval of others, and it would be awful to let people down", for example), before we dispute it at D. What if we had stopped at "missing an open goal" and taken this as the critical A? We are no nearer to the centre of Kelly's shame if we do this because she is not ashamed about the missed penalty per se, it is specifically the *inferred* social-evaluative features ("letting people down") of that event that is leading to this shame, alongside her irrational beliefs about letting people down. We cannot assume the client holds irrational beliefs about the first A they present to us, else we construct the client's issue inaccurately and thus form inaccurate solutions.

Finally, what is also apparent in the dialogue with Kelly is that some potential As are concrete (i.e., reflecting confirmable reality), some are perceptions of reality (i.e., presumed to be the case) and some are inferential (i.e., conclusions about what has been perceived; DiGiuseppe et al., 2014). Concrete As could be "stuttering" and "my boss, colleagues, juniors, saw it", perceived As could be "everybody saw me do it" and "They've supported me and given me opportunities", and inferential As could be "Well, they probably judged me. They probably questioned my ability" and "I've let them all down". In REBT, whether these As are *actually* true or not, the client reacts to them emotionally so the practitioner considers them to be true (DiGiuseppe et al., 2014). As such, in specific REBT we would not dispute these As before we have disputed the Bs.

In conversing with the client, you will uncover these A layers (concrete As, perceived As, inferential As) and will have to distinguish which As are germane and most proximal to the client issues and are triggering of Bs. In any situation there are many facets that can be attended to, few of which are perceived, and even fewer of which lead to inferences (e.g., Wessler & Wessler, 1980). But one of these inferences will be particularly important because it triggers B – this inference, the critical A, is the aspect of the situation that the client then applies their irrational beliefs to, taking a "bad" event to an "awful" event, for example.

Another complimentary strategy for assessing A and finding the critical A is to present the client with the As that have been discussed, and to ask them which A they are most disturbed (e.g., anxious, angry, ashamed) about. So, in the Kelly example the practitioner could ask, "Are you most ashamed of missing the open goal, being judged, or letting people down?" In my experience, as you take the client deeper into the As, getting closer to the critical A and the irrational beliefs, often the client will experience, or begin to experience, the relevant associated emotion in the session. For example, Kelly might start to avoid eye contact with the practitioner and may become visibly withdrawn (e.g., closed body language, slumped shoulders), and may be slow to respond to questions. The perceptive practitioner will treat this rise in emotionality as a sign that they are on the right track, but caution must be applied. Haphazardly facilitating a journey into disturbance could damage the working alliance, and may instigate some distrust. The practitioner should tread carefully, but still pursue this line of enquiry with a view to helping the client to address the UNE through REBT work.

Assume A is true

Of all I have learned studying and applying REBT, the principle of "assume A is true" has served me best and changed the way I interact with clients. For example, a client might say "my boss totally ignored me at work yesterday" which might be an accurate representation of events, or it could be a perception (inaccurate or accurate). Taking the stance that "what the client says at A is true" is more likely to help us with a specific REBT solution whereby B becomes the focus of the disputation, rather than A. The practitioner could spend lots of precious session time questioning the veracity of the perception that the boss ignored the client. Maybe she did, but was having a bad day so can be excused. Maybe she didn't and the client is laying some bias over the situation. It might be a mixture of both of these potential occurrences, it might be neither, but why speculate? Why not just respect the client's perspective on this A and treat what they say as true? If we challenge every A, then the work will go nowhere, the client will incorrectly assume that As are the root of their UNEs, and they may even go on the defensive because their perceptions are constantly being challenged (Neenan & Dryden, 1996). The client feels better in the short-term thinking that they have not been treated poorly, but this is no long-term solution for the irrational beliefs at the root of the UNE, and will not fortify them against future transgressions (perceived or actual). In REBT we can encourage the client to assume the worst and feel healthy, adaptive, but still negative, emotions even if the concrete, perceived, and inferential As were true (DiGiuseppe et al., 2014). So, for REBT it is more fruitful and efficient to assume A to be true and to work towards understanding what the source of the UNE is; specifically the irrational belief/s. Fruitful because we can address what is underpinning the UNE, and efficient because we won't be challenging and addressing every non-critical A. We know that A is contributing to the emotion, but that it is unlikely to be the source of the UNE alone, and importantly, once undisturbed, the client can address the A if necessary, but from a place of rationality.

For other useful techniques for finding the critical A, the reader could consult Dryden's work on the subject (1989, 2009b, 2019b, 2022), and for a detailed discussion and examples of inference chaining, the reader should consult Neenan and Dryden (1996). Further reading and training is important because some critical As can be arrived at quite simply, while others require some dedicated teasing out.

Summary

In this chapter I discussed the A element of the GABCDE framework. I defined what As are and nested potential As in themes that could guide assessment. I also covered inference chaining, the importance of locating and establishing the critical A, and introduced some client examples in order to help illustrate some A assessment. Given that we now have an understanding of A and C, next I will move onto a fundamental concern in REBT but one that has been seldom written about in detail – the goals (G).

6 Goals (G)

Ellis considered human beings to be, biologically and by social learning, goal seeking animals, and in REBT goals are fundamental to being (Ellis, 1994). Indeed, every aspect of the GABCDE framework is relevant to the goals of the client, in keeping with the interdependent nature of the framework. When I speak of goals here, I do not mean the goals of the work we are doing together in the sessions (i.e., therapy goals or aims). This is commonly used by other authors, which is fine. But here I refer to goals in a similar way to how Ellis (1994) referred to goals, whereby humans have fundamental goals (FGs; to survive, to assuage unnecessary pain, to be fulfilled), and primary/sub-goals (PGs; to be satisfied; alone, socially (including intimately with some), informationally/educationally, vocationally, economically, and recreationally). We can work with clients to articulate exactly what needs to be done to attain the PGs that underpin and serve their FGs.

Explicit in REBT are the broad human goals of living this life with as much enjoyment as possible, living peacefully within our chosen group, and relating intimately with certain people of our choosing (DiGiuseppe et al., 2014). Ellis (1994) added human goals of reason and logic, success in solving and mastering life problems and meaningful tasks, experiencing new and stimulating things, and stability/security in work and social life. These broad goals "provide a context that affects how people perceive their activating events and how they evaluate the world" (Crawford & Ellis, 1989, p. 3). Importantly, these goals are preferences and desires, not needs or necessities, and rationality should be in service of these short- and long-term goals (Nelson-Jones, 2006). Importantly, perceived or anticipated goal attainment usually leads to positive emotion, and perceived or anticipated threats to goal attainment usually leads to negative emotions (e.g., Frijda, 1986, 1988), which of course is in line with the work of Lazarus (1999) as discussed earlier in the book. In brief, when people evaluate A as congruent with or helpful towards their goals (G), they generally experience positively valenced emotions at C. But when people evaluate A as incongruent with or sabotaging their goals (G), they generally experience negatively valenced emotions at C. Enter Ellis and REBT. If these people then make a choice, consciously or unconsciously, to apply *irrational* beliefs to this G-A incongruence, then UNEs are likely, If, however, these people make a choice to apply *rational* beliefs to the G-A incongruence, then HNEs are likely.

DOI: 10.4324/9781003508472-7

Because people are goal-driven, at times (inevitably) unfortunate and undesirable occurrences (As), will interfere with the attainment of these goals (Ellis, 1994; Shea, 2016), because we are limited and fallible beings, and our environment is unpredictable, uncertain, and (largely) uncontrollable. Put another way, people are goal-driven consciously and unconsciously, and therefore will run into adversities (As) that impede and threaten their goals, such is the human condition (fallible, limited) and such is life (uncontrollable, unpredictable, uncertain). As such, G and A are related in REBT, because A is adverse to the extent that it is incongruent with G. Because emotions are reactions to action outcomes (obstructed or facilitated) in relation to an individual's goals (Carver & Scheier, 1998; Frijda, 1986; Kreibig et al., 2010), G and A create the conditions for emotional consequences (C). The pursuit of meaningful Gs can bring about negative emotions because by pursuing these goals one will undoubtedly face challenges, barriers, and setbacks because the world, and the people you engage with and contend with, are not predictable, controllable, or wholly benign. In other words, having Gs brings about As. Your humanness, limited and imperfect, means that your pursuit of meaningful Gs will be met with some challenges to overcome, some pain, some suffering.

When people experience or infer A, whether and to what extent A impedes or is inimical to G, and the nature of this impediment, plays a significant role in determining the emotion at C, with the application of rational or irrational beliefs (B) to G and or A establishing either HNEs or UNEs. Goals (G) underpin the desires that formulate preferences (or "wants"), which people can then apply demandingness (or "musts") to. People can have preferential desires (primary rational beliefs), or demanding desires (primary irrational beliefs; Ellis et al., 2010). The more strongly you hold desires at G, the more affecting As will be, and the more likely you are to experience UNEs when holding irrational beliefs (B).

For example, a dancer wants to achieve a full and illustrious career (G), but sustains a career-shortening injury (non-critical A). This A could clearly generate many additional As and the practitioner would work with the client to identify the critical A. But say the critical A is, "I have spent my entire life pursuing this career, for nothing". The client can choose to rationally believe that "I want to, but I don't have to, have a full and illustrious career, and even though my life's pursuit has now ended, it does not mean that I am a complete failure". Or they can choose to irrationally believe that "I want to, and therefore I must, have a full and illustrious career, and because my life's pursuit has now ended, I am a complete and utter failure". The rational belief is likely to underpin sadness (HNE), whereas the irrational belief is likely to underpin depression (non-clinical; UNE). We can make this assumption about the nature of C based on the information in Figure 5.2 where the Ellisian meets the Lazarusian, but of course we would undertake a detailed discursive C assessment with the client to fully understand the precise C related to the apparent G-A incongruence.

People covertly and overtly sneak musts into their Gs, As, Bs (and Cs), and they importantise their Gs (Ellis, 1994) which appears to justify their musts ("Because G is so very important, then I simply must achieve it"). It is important to state that the client's Gs maybe explicit or implicit in the work that you do with them, but As are problematic to the extent that they are perceived to impede the client's Gs. In other words, the presence of A implies the existence of G. The perceived impediment at A does not necessarily mean that the client will not achieve those goals. But the application of irrational beliefs and the likely experience of UNEs will not help, and will probably hinder and undermine, the client's efforts to achieve those goals (Browne et al., 2010).

The importance of G

Clients often come with problems at A or at C, and we can gain greater insight into just how problematic A and C are, by understanding G. In other words, we can figure out precisely what A and C are prohibiting the client from achieving. We can better understand the nature of the client's problems against the backdrop of their goals, and particularly, how these goals are being, or will be, thwarted by A. This allows greater specificity when seeking and articulating client irrational beliefs, because we can be mindful of both G and A and the incongruence that specific As present to specific Gs. So, a thorough A and G assessment is ideal in order to gain a full picture of the client's issues. Also, understating G allows us to put A in context, and helps the client figure out which Cs would be useful in fulfilling G. That is, we can help the client formulate and articulate the HNEs that would serve their G attainment in light of the As they will face. So, establishing G is important in situations where the client is seeking our help with an A or C (which is usually the case). If we want to help clients to achieve their goals, then we *and they* need to know what those goals are.

As an example of the GABCDE inclusive of FGs and PGs, let's take the client who experiences a career-shortening injury and assume that they have come to a decision to transition out their performing career into a teaching role. We can map out some potential As, Bs, Cs, and also throw some Ds into the mix:

FG To be fulfilled in life. To fulfil one's potential as a human being.

PG Develop a new and fruitful career in teaching that sustains me vocationally and economically

As Transition, failure, sacrifice (time, effort, and money), judgement, uncertainty, rejection, unfairness.

UNEs Unhealthy anxiety, unhealthy anger, shame.

iBs I really want to and therefore I must have a fruitful teaching career, and I cannot stand barriers to this goal, impediments would be terrible, and if I don't achieve this it would make me a complete failure.

D[1] Where is the evidence for these beliefs? Are they consistent with reality? What function do these beliefs serve?

rB I really want to have a fruitful teaching career, but I don't have to. When barriers to this goal emerge, it will be tough but I can stand it, impediments would be inconvenient but certainly not terrible, and if I don't achieve this, it just shows that I am a fallible human being and can accept myself fully as that.

D^2 Where is the evidence for these beliefs? Are they consistent with reality? What function do these beliefs serve?

HNEs Healthy anxiety, healthy anger, disappointment.

In the above example, one can see how the nature of the Gs gives rise to particular As, which as result activates some irrational beliefs (iBs), leading to some unhealthy Cs. We can, as REBT practitioners, then help the client to challenge and dispute (D) the iBs, and develop (and of course equally challenge and dispute) some rBs, leading to healthy Cs. It is not possible to be specific about the details of ABC without having an accurate and detailed understanding of G. Obtain these details includes encouraging clients to be specific about the details of their goals. We can ask, "what does a fulfilled life look like to you?", "how will you know you have fulfilled your human potential?" (FGs), and "what exactly would a fruitful and sustaining teaching career look like", "how will you know you have attained a fruitful and sustaining teaching career?" (PGs). We can encourage the client to envision the future them, having attained these FGs and PGs, so that we can gain some important specifics regarding these goals. Obviously, this line of questioning is not to be rushed, and it might be the first time the client has ever been asked to think about and articulate their FGs in this way.

Helping the client to identify their goal/s is of utmost importance, because we create our world via what we strive towards and the aims we set (Ellis et al., 2010). Ellis (1991) indicated that "to make a stable habit of full functioning, one had better consciously choose the goal or purpose of becoming fully functioning" (p. 187). Far be it for us to tell clients what they *should* and *should not* work towards. Indeed, it is not possible or appropriate for the practitioner to specify a goal *for* a client, particularly the FG, as it should reflect their personal values. However, we can help clients to ask themselves the right questions concerning their goals (e.g., Ellis, 1991), such as:

- What do I really like and dislike?
- What do I want and not want?
- How can I experiment and discover what I truly like and dislike?
- Which of my likes and dislikes will probably harm me long-term?
- What am I likely to prefer and abhor in the future?
- What do I want to move towards?
- What do I want to move away from?
- What do I do to enhance my likes and decrease my dislikes?
- How can I align my options more closely to the data of my experiences?
- How can I align my short-term goals with my longer-term goals?
- How can I align my PGs with my FGs?

As humanistic practitioners applying REBT, the whole person should be considered not just the role-related expression of the person (i.e., "Dancer", "Manager",

"Teacher"). REBT has always been about helping the person as a whole, not just confined aspects of who they are (e.g., job roles). Thus, when we are interacting with clients about their goals, we are careful not to constrain this conversation to the domain in which they currently reside. When we are discussing FGs, we are seeking to unearth and articulate deeper goals that drive the client, that speaks to fulfilment as a human being. To do this, we can help the client to gain some clarity on a) the composition of their core values, b) what they believe their inner potential is, and c) what fulfilment would look like to *them*.

Although generally we would not challenge a client's preferences and desires, it is useful to do so if it is clear for client and practitioner that these preferences and desires might be introjected (taken from others without consideration) or false (Dryden, 2012c). Sometimes, the goals a client holds have been transacted onto them by people around them, and these goals do not speak to what they *actually* want from life or will lead to their fulfilment. So, we can help clients to wisely work towards FGs rather than unwisely working towards superficial, facile, introjected goals such as fortune and fame, momentary happiness and short-term pleasure. Indeed,

> short range hedonism – eat, drink, and be merry, for tomorrow you may die! – has its distinct limitations, for tomorrow you will probably be alive with the hangover!. . . immediate gratification had often better be avoided and long-range hedonism sought out and abetted.
>
> (Ellis, 1991, p. 193)

FGs and PGs

By identifying an FG, we can encourage clients to consider the bigger picture, and look beyond what they desire as part of their PGs, to what they would like to move towards as an FG. The PGs are more likely to be imbued with meaning and purpose if they are in service of the FG. Therefore, we can ask the client, "Is the PG in service of the FG?" In other words, does the PG help the client move towards the FG? Instead of asking the client "what do you desire?", we can ask "what do you want to move towards?", and "what PGs in life would help you move towards your FG?".

It is the current author's view, also echoed in Ellis' (1994) view of FGs and PGs, that a PG such as vocational satisfaction (e.g., work achievement), should not be confused for an FG. In other words, vocational success (PG) should not be the underpinning fundamental goal (FG) for human beings, but should be in service of the broader and grander FG that transcends work, hobbies, economics – i.e., is eudaimonic and reflects core values. This is not to denigrate the endeavours that constitute PGs, but human beings are more than the roles they play at work, and are certainly more than their bank balance. This PG and FG distinction is important, in part, because the attainment of PGs are dependent on external factors; the Stoics warn against overvaluing external things, because they are outside of our control. Work success, for example, is dependent on various internal *and* external factors, thus evading our total volition. For example, while is it nice to be approved of, yearning for approval and making it our FG in life is dangerous especially if we unwisely sneak demands for approval into this desire. We can't control it, and we certainly don't "need" it, so why would we make it an FG? Nobody can bestow our FG upon us; eudaimonia is self-generated, it comes from within, and come from truth, reason, integrity, and wisdom, is autonomous – it depends only on itself (Robertson, 2019). So, clients are encouraged to pursue PGs but not at the cost of FGs, which are primary and paramount.

To be clear, it is not that I am saying that clients should not seek success in their pursuits, whatever that looks like for them. I issue a caution against overvaluing goals that are not within the client's control, confusing PGs for FGs. Too much importance placed on PGs can lead to a fusing of the self with the endeavour, making it dangerous to fail or face setbacks. In other words, self-worth becomes conditional on the achievement of said goal. I cover this idea in more detail in a later chapter, but suffice it to say that as a result, you (the self) become trapped in your endeavour and will find it more difficult to stand up to wrongdoing or step away from it when necessary. This is because you do not want to jeopardize the goal you have placed as your FG, which you have attached your self-worth to – "If I transition away from work, who am I?". When a PG is erroneously placed as an FG, the genuine FG is less likely to be attained because it has been overshadowed by the PG, and thus the pursuit of the proper FG has been neglected. In short, dissuade clients from staking their self-worth as a human being on their goal pursuits.

Rational goal pursuit

Once the goals have been articulated (ideally as PGs and FGs), then the practitioner can help the client to orient their lives towards the goals, employing problem solving concerning As, Bs and Cs. As the client strives towards the goal, and more information and clarity comes to light concerning the ABCs, we can help the client to reformulate their solutions flexibly, holding the belief that

> it would be nice if I was able to achieve my goals without any hiccups, but that doesn't mean that I have to, and while it is tough, I can certainly tolerate the many barriers and setbacks that might come my way on the way to my goals.

In addition, as the client meets PGs and shorter-term goals, this will influence their conceptualization of future PGs. I have seen it so often with the people I work with. The client at one time believes that in achieving a particular short-term goal that they will be satisfied, only to find that meeting this goal opens up a range of other possible goals. In this chapter, I have argued that, regardless of specific PGs and short-term goals, the continuous forward movement towards FGs is a life-long endeavour.

Summary

In REBT, we consider human beings to be goal-driven, and we can help clients to pursue many personal and professional goals ('PGs'), underpinned by eudaimonic (long-term life fulfilment) and meaning-laden goals ('FGs'). Because of the chaotic and unpredictable world clients inhabit, they will face many adversities (A) in pursuit of their goals, and will necessarily suffer as a result, especially emotionally (C). Clients who pursue their goals through the development and application of rationality, are more likely to experience HNEs rather than UNEs in the face of adversity (A). Thus, clients able to check and challenge their perceptions of the world, understand what is and is not with their control, and hone their rational beliefs, can fortify themselves against the adversities that will occur as a result of their pursuit towards meaningful goals. In other words, rationality can help clients to pursue what is meaningful, readying them to forthrightly face the inevitable vicissitudes of life, without sacrificing their mental and physical health as they do so.

In REBT, we can help the client to a) articulate and orient themselves towards FGs and PGs, b) problem solve at A, c) address potential irrational beliefs that could bring about UNEs, d) bolster potential rational beliefs that could bring about HNEs, and e) use the GABCDE framework and the "rules" of REBT, including how to use disputation (D) on their own rigid and extreme beliefs. As such, the GABCDE framework can be used remedially, and proactively. In other words, a deeper and shared understanding of G will aid the client and I in dealing with a past, current or future known As, and aid a proactive forward-thinking approach to goal pursuit by taking reasonable steps to dealing with future unknown potential As. We can help clients to prepare and train for the arduous endeavour of goal pursuit. By learning how to use the GABCDE framework proactively, the client gains some autonomy over their goal pursuit, including the emotion regulation that will surely have to take place as they pursue this goal. As Ellis (1991) notes, "with self-actualization: Only by working at planning, plotting, scheming and steadily acting at it are you likely to become a fully-functioning person" (p. 193).

7 Beliefs (B) in rational emotive behaviour therapy

There are many things that I want in life, and because I want them so very much, then I simply must have them. If I don't get what I want, then I would not be able to bear it, and it would not just be bad, it would be terrible. My not getting what I want would go to illustrate that I am a useless idiot, and that the world is a rotten place, and so are the people in it.

The above piece captures the four core irrational beliefs of REBT, and you may recognize some of this language from the clients you work with, people you surround yourself with, and indeed, from your own internal dialogue. These four core irrational beliefs will be covered in detail in this chapter, after some discussion about the concept of rationality at the heart of REBT, and the notion of belief.

Rationality in REBT

In REBT, rationality is aligned with what Keith Stanovich (2012) calls the "stronger sense" (p. 344) of rationality. Specifically, "Rationality (and irrationality) comes in degrees defined by the distance of the thought or behaviour from the optimum defined by a normative model" (p. 344). Stanovich, whose contribution to the study and understanding of rationality is substantial, describes two types of rationality; Epistemic (evidential, theoretical) rationality which concerns how well beliefs map onto the actual structure of the world, and instrumental rationality which concerns behaving in the world so that you get exactly what you most want, given the resources (physical and mental) available to you. These types of rationality are clearly within the remit of rationality as held in REBT, with a congruence in characteristics of empirical, logical, and functional elements to rationality. Stanovich et al. (2008) suggest that we could characterize instrumental rationality as the optimization of the individual's goal fulfilment, aligning REBT even more closely with Stanovich's representation of rationality, and also aligns with Stephen Pinker's (2021) writing about rationality. Pinker offers that rationality "is a kit of cognitive tools that can attain particular goals in particular worlds" (p. 7), is "the ability to use knowledge to attain goals" (p. 36), and suggest we "ground our beliefs in truth" (p. 37). While perfect rationality should be striven for, it is an aspiration

DOI: 10.4324/9781003508472-8

that no mortal human can attain (Pinker, 2021). What we try to do in REBT is help clients develop this "rational kit of cognitive tools" (i.e., beliefs) in service of their goals, all the while knowing and understanding that people will not and cannot always think and act rationally. REBT constrains its definitions of "rational" and "irrational" by suggesting that rationality is explicitly counter to irrationality. This is why, for example, rational preferences include the negation of demands.

Beliefs

Why are beliefs important? Perhaps Mahatma Gandhi said it best: "Your beliefs become your thoughts, Your thoughts become your words, Your words become your actions, your actions become your habits, Your habits become your values, Your values become your destiny". In REBT, we do not speak of rationality as a nebulous construct or a lofty philosophical way of life, we speak of rational beliefs and irrational beliefs. But what is a belief in REBT? The concept of belief in REBT aligns with the viewpoints proffered by a great many authors, and a fill discussion can be found in Turner (2022). But in brief, within REBT, beliefs are deeply held (tacit) propositions, assumptions, rules, ideas, attitudes, sets of expectations, ways of seeing the world that have cognitive, emotional and behavioural concomitants and consequences. They are considered to be enduring, contextual (they are often *about* something), and can exist as tacit-like schemata and or as deliberative evaluations. But, and it's a big "but", beliefs are subject to change through rigorous discursive and experiential means. More on that later in this book, but specifically, in REBT, the notion of beliefs is contextualized within the ideas of rationality and irrationality, which are precisely defined with explicit conceptual boundaries and borders.

Rational beliefs are propositions, assumptions, rules, ideas, attitudes, ways of seeing the world, that are scientifically warranted, flexible, non-extreme, and usually underpin human survival and fulfilment, at least more so than irrational beliefs which are unscientific, rigid, and absolutistic, and undercut human survival and well-being (Ellis, 1987a; Ellis & MacLaren, 1998; Robb, 2003). In other words, in REBT rational means self-helping and irrational means self-defeating, and as such the chief aims of REBT is to help people weaken their irrational beliefs and strengthen their rational beliefs (Ellis & Dryden, 1997). But let me be balanced here and repeat Ellis' assertion, "beliefs that are scientifically warranted are **usually rational** in the sense that they **normally** lead to human survival and happiness – or at least **do so more often** than do unscientific, absolutistic beliefs" (Ellis, 1987a, p. 137). The bold elements illustrate that it is not the case that *all* scientifically unwarranted beliefs are dysfunctional for goal attainment.

Irrational beliefs have the characteristics of: being absolute, dichotomous, rigid, and unbending; illogical; inconsistent with reality; not helpful to achieve one's goal; lead to unhealthy/dysfunctional emotions. In contrast, rational beliefs have the characteristics of being: flexible; logical; consistent with reality; helpful in pursuing one's goal; lead to healthy/functional emotions, even when the person is facing negative events (e.g., DiGiuseppe et al., 2014). More broadly, irrational beliefs are cognitive expressions of the unwillingness to accept an unwanted outcome related to one's striving to achieve something positive or to block something negative. In addition, irrational beliefs are unscientific in part because they offer many propositions that are unfalsifiable (Still, 2010). Rational beliefs are cognitive expressions of the basic willingness to accept an unwanted outcome of reality related to one's striving to achieve something positive or to block something negative, regardless of how much it deviates from what one wants and independent of how strong one's desire is (DiGiuseppe et al., 2014), and are falsifiable. Vitally, irrational beliefs underpin unhealthy negative emotions (UNEs), and rational beliefs underpin healthy negative emotions (HNEs).

> "*It is undesirable to believe a proposition when there is no ground whatever for supposing it true. I must, of course, admit that if such an opinion became common it would completely transform our social life and our political system*"
>
> -Bertrand Russell

Put simply, rational beliefs refer to "beliefs that are logical, and/or have empirical support, and/or are pragmatic" and irrational beliefs are "beliefs that are illogical, and/or do not have empirical support, and/or are nonpragmatic" (Ellis et al., 2010, p. 3). As can be seen by the use of "and/or", a belief need not fit all three criteria to be rational, but it is necessary that a belief meet at least one criterion, or a combination of criteria (Ellis et al., 2010). As such, rational beliefs in part are defined in line with scientific and intellectual thought, in that they are logically consistent and supported by empirical evidence. But importantly, rational beliefs also enable people to achieve their goals (Wilson, 2010). It is therefore useful to consider rational and irrational beliefs to be defined psychologically rather than philosophically (Ellis et al., 2010), because after all, it is the development and enhancement of human functioning that is at the centre of REBT, not just logic for logic's sake. Indeed, rational beliefs are usually self-enhancing (Dryden, 2017), and often underpin HNEs (DiGiuseppe et al., 2014), while in contrast irrational beliefs are usually unhelpful in pursuing, and inconsistent with accomplishing, one's long-term goals (i.e., they are self-defeating; Dryden, 2017; Maultsby, 1975), and often underpin UNEs (DiGiuseppe et al., 2014).

Rational beliefs: Beliefs that are logical, and/or have empirical support, and/or are pragmatic

Irrational beliefs: Beliefs that are illogical, and/or do not have empirical support, and/or are nonpragmatic

What are the rational and irrational beliefs of REBT?

In REBT, there are four core rational beliefs and four core irrational beliefs (see Ellis et al., 2010, for in-depth discussions). The rational beliefs are full preferences, anti-awfulizing, frustration tolerance (FT), and unconditional acceptance (self; USA, other; OUA, world; WUA). The irrational beliefs are demandingness, awfulizing, frustration intolerance (FI), and self, other, life/world depreciation/ global evaluation (GE). The way that I see the structure of rational and irrational beliefs in REBT is through a superordinate, subordinate, and basic system. *Superordinate* (high level, highly abstract) are the categories of "irrational" and "rational". *Subordinate* to each superordinate category are the core beliefs namely preferences, anti-awfulizing, frustration tolerance (FT), and USA, OUA, WUA (subordinate to "rational"), and demandingness, awfulizing, frustration intolerance (FI), and self, other, life/world depreciation/GE (subordinate to "irrational"). Then, at the basic level (low abstraction) are the specific articulated beliefs held by the client which are particular to their either Gs and or As (e.g., "I want to, and therefore I must, play professional football", "being mistreated by my boss is not just bad, it is awful").

My aim in the rest of this chapter is to introduce and detail the four core irrational/rational beliefs of REBT. I move through each belief pairing thusly:

- Demandingness (e.g., "I want to achieve my goals, and therefore I absolutely must") versus preferences (e.g., "I want to achieve my goals, but that does not mean that I must")
- Frustration intolerance (e.g., "I cannot tolerate being treated unfairly") versus frustration tolerance (e.g., "Being treated unfairly is difficult to tolerate, but I can certainly tolerate it, and it is worth it to do so")
- Awfulizing (e.g., "underperforming is not just bad, it is truly awful") versus anti-awfulizing (e.g., "underperformance is bad, but certainly not *awful*")
- Depreciation (global evaluation) (e.g., "because I have not been selected for promotion, it shows that I am a completely worthless person") versus unconditional acceptance (e.g., "not being selected for promotion is not ideal, but it does not make me a worthless person – it just shows that I am a fallible human being, just like everyone else")

Demandingness versus preferences

In light of individual goals, people's desires first include partial preferences (e.g., DiGiuseppe et al., 2014; Dryden, 2009a; Ellis et al., 2010) such as "I want to perform well in things that matter to me". A full rational preference belief would be "I want to perform well in things that matter to me, but that does not mean that I must". For a full preference, a negation of the demand is present. This is important because the practitioner needs to know whether the preference is merely a preference, or whether the preference is a precursor to a demand, for example, "I want to perform well in things that matter to me, and therefore I must". That is, people's desires first include wishes and preferences ("I *want to* perform well") but then may also include absolutistic demands ("I *have to* perform well"). So, the architecture of a full rational preference includes the preference and the negation of a demand, while an irrational demand (demandingness) includes the preference transformed into a demand (Dryden, 2009a). This delineation is not trivial. Often the client will express a partial preference and the demand is implicit. It is our job as the practitioner to elucidate whether the partial preference is just that or whether a demand is being applied to the preference.

Demandingness is where one turns a preference into an absolutistic demand (Armstrong, 2017). By turning "wants" into "musts", which are exaggerated and unrealistic (Ellis, 2003a), secondary irrational beliefs can quickly follow (e.g., "I want to and therefore I must succeed, else it would be unbearable, and I'd be a useless loser"), which contributes to unhealthy patterns of emotional and behavioural functioning. In REBT, it is when people escalate preferences into demands that UNEs are more likely to occur (Ellis et al., 2010). Human desires are usually healthy and productive but demands (musts, have tos, absolutely shoulds, needs) are often unhealthy and destructive. Ultimately, we are asking, "does a demand logically follow from a preference?" and we are answering, "no, it does not" (e.g., Still, 2010). Ellis (2002b) points out that it is strong desires rather than weak desires that we are more likely to apply demands to. For example, "Because succeeding is so important and desirable for me, then I absolutely must succeed". Ellis (2002b) describes this transferring of wants to musts as grandiose and perfectionistic, because obviously I don't run the universe, so whatever I desire, no matter how strongly I *want* it, doesn't *have to* exist.

A good example of separating "want" from "must" is apparent in an interview given to Sky Sports by Jurgen Klopp (Manager of Liverpool Football Club, English Premier League Champions 2020) about an upcoming (important) match against Manchester City Football Club. Here is an excerpt:

Interviewer: Given where you are in the table, the gap is six point right now, you're the team leading the table. For you, is it more of a "must not lose" as opposed to a "must win" game?

Klopp: (laughing) I am sorry, it is because maybe there are other people who are smarter than me and can see it this, I don't see it like this. For me its 100% a *want to win* game.

Interviewer: *Want* to win . . .

Klopp: (nodding head) *Want* to win. 100% with all I have, and erm, this must win "must" thing I never understood because that doesn't change the chances.

Klopp goes on to reaffirm that "we want to win, and we try everything we can make that happen, which is difficult enough". This philosophy does not appear to have done him any harm, despite the importance of the match (he got a 3–1 victory in the match, and won the premier league title that season).

Transferring a preference into a demand is an example of a non-sequitur, where a conclusion does not follow logically from a previous statement. So, "therefore I must" does not logically follow on from "I want to succeed". Just because you want to succeed, does not mean that you must. Thus, demanding what you prefer is not consistent with reality – it is just not how the world works. Indeed, the "essence of psychological health in REBT theory is rational acceptance of reality" (Ziegler, 2003, p. 28), so beliefs that are inconsistent with reality, i.e., to demand that things be as one would like them to be, is a non-starter. To hold non-sequitur beliefs is to abandon the Stoic ideal of living in accord with reason. While of course it makes sense that a client would want to be competent, respected, valued, etc., demanding that they must be competent, respected, valued, etc. (a) does not make it more likely, (b) propels these "wants" into existential necessities thus exacerbating the emotional consequences of facing inevitable barriers (As) to these desires, and (c) is empirically false, since there is no rule or empirical law that dictates they "must" get what they want (Still, 2010). Dryden (2019a) points out that if the demand "I want X to happen and therefore it must" were true, then it would be impossible for X not to be happen, but of course it *is* possible for X not to be happen. In other words, "if something, as a matter of fact, absolutely must, or had to be, a certain way, then that is the way it would be. The *fact* that it is not that way proves the assertion is wrong" (Robb, 2003, p. 36). Clients who demand success on the basis of their desire to succeed only need to reflect for a few seconds before that can recall a time when they have not succeeded, thus undermining their demand. Ellis (2002a) states that "By making your strong desires into "necessities" you tend to sabotage rather than aid in the achievement of your goals" (p. 18).

So it is the "want" becoming a "must" that is self-destructive and dysfunctional and defines "demandingness". Preferences align with our goals, which makes sense because humans tend to move towards that which we desire. But when that which we desire becomes a demand, a must, a have to, the consequences of not getting what we desire becomes a perceived existential threat, and thus is too much to bear, is awful, and shows that we are failures. So, we approach the desire with desperation and panic, and when we don't get what we want, we understandably become emotionally distressed. Dryden (2012c) suggests that a partial preferential belief (e.g., "I really want to be selected for the job") followed by "but I do not have to be" can be considered a full preferential belief. But if the partial preferential belief (e.g., "I really want to be selected for the job") is followed by "and therefore I must be", then this reflects the belief's transformation into demandingness. By making sure the client states the full preferential belief, not just the partial preferential belief, we make it unlikely that demandingness will occur. In other words, don't just let the client articulate a preference without negating the demand.

So, when working with demandingness, the practitioner should consider the preferential derivation of the demand, the conditionality of the demand, and relatedly, the logical validity of the condition if one is present. Ellis (2002a) suggests that irrational, unconditional musts, contain no "buts", while rational preferences have "buts" either stated or implied – "I would like to be selected, but I do not have to be". Irrational demands are absolute – no buts. I encourage the practitioner to consider four questions when distinguishing demands:

1. Is the demand absolute (no buts)?
2. Is the demand based on a preference (I *want and therefore* I must)?
3. Is the demand conditional (in order to y, I must x)? If there is a condition, is the condition logically valid (x evidently leads to y)?
4. Is the demand helping or harming goal attainment and or fulfilment?

If the answers to these questions are yes (1), yes (2), no (3), and "harming" (4), then it appears that the irrational demandingness belief in question is a very good candidate for disputation (D).

Frustration Intolerance (FI) versus Frustration Tolerance (FT)

Frustration intolerance (FI) beliefs are where a person holds an extreme belief that they cannot stand, tolerate, bear, the adversity they are facing or will face (Dryden, 2019a). For example, a client might believe that "I cannot stand being rejected by peers" or "I can't bear my boss treating me unfairly". In contrast, frustration tolerance (FT) beliefs are where a person holds a flexible belief that it is difficult to tolerate the adversity they are facing or will face, but they can tolerate it and it is worth it to do so (Dryden, 2019a). For example a client might believe that "It is difficult to tolerate being rejected by peers, but I can tolerate it and it is worth doing so" or "It is tough to bear my boss treating me unfairly, but I can bear it and it is worth it to do so".

In some contexts, it might be important to hold a belief that "I *will not* tolerate this person treating me this way" *alongside* "I *can* tolerate this person treating me this way". In other words, although I *can* tolerate the ill treatment, I chose not to. This *will* to, and *will* not to, tolerate adversity could be functional especially for example if the client perceives potential abuse from a boss, or a colleague. There is a difference between the ability to tolerate, and the will to tolerate, and clients should certainly work on their ability to tolerate ALL adversities, but retain the choice to not tolerate adversity (e.g., "I *can* tolerate you treating me this way, but I *will not* tolerate it"). This enables remonstration and activism if appropriate. The fact that the client *is* tolerating something is evidence that they *can* tolerate it, but *is* and *can* do not mean *will* or *ought*. This really comes back to an earlier point in the book about changing A. Of course, at times in REBT we can encourage clients to change the situation they are in (or avoid particularly dangerous situations), in other words changing A. But clients will be more equipped to change A if they approach this A change rationally, whereby they are thinking, feeling, and behaving in a functional manner. You can better assert yourself with a transgressor if you are not boiling over with rage (or unhealthy anger). In relation to FT, successful A change might include believing that you *can* tolerate A, but choosing not to tolerate it by taking action to change A.

FI beliefs are non-sequiturs, in the sense that just because something is difficult or tough, does not mean that it is intolerable. Just because a client is finding a situation to be difficult or frustrating (i.e., adverse), this does not mean that they *cannot stand* it or *cannot bear* it. It might be the toughest thing they have ever faced; it still doesn't qualify the extreme FI belief. Indeed, often people report that they "cannot stand" what they do not like (DiGiuseppe et al., 2014). When a person holds an FI belief, they believe that if what they desire does not happen, they will die or disintegrate, and or will lose their capacity to experience happiness (Dryden, 2019a). FI beliefs are also clearly factually or empirically false when used to describe past or current adversity. The lack of evidence that a person cannot tolerate a past or current adversity lays within the fact of their continued existence made apparent by their presence at the REBT session. In other words, evidence for the FT belief, and against the FI belief, is confirmed by the fact that the client is sitting before you, and has obviously tolerated the adversity, on account of them not being deceased. For FI that concerns future adversity (e.g., "my boss is going to scold me for this mistake, and I can't stand it when that happens"), the client only needs to spend a minute or so recalling tough (perhaps similar) situations of the past to realize that they have stood equal or worse adversities, and are thus capable of standing the upcoming adversity (real or imagined).

Is it worth it?

A hallmark of FT beliefs is the notion that the adversity is worth tolerating. It is of course more than likely that by tolerating the adversity the client will grow and develop, finding meaning in the adversity that would be unexplored if they were not faced with the adversity. Human beings are capable of tremendous antifragility (Taleb, 2012), which is the property to increase capability and thrive as a result of stressors. I take the stance that whether and what extent the adversity is worth tolerating is down to the client to decide (we can of course help with the decision); lest the client push themselves into situations that could result in actual harm. But this should not allay efforts to work towards FT beliefs. Even if the adversity it not worth tolerating (e.g., tolerating the adversity is not advantageous for goal attainment or well-being), it is still a good idea for the client to believe that they *could* or *can* tolerate the adversity if they chose to. That is, it is advantageous to believe that you are capable of tolerating an adversity, whether you decide to tolerate it or not. Indeed, FT beliefs are in part underscored by the belief that you have a choice to tolerate the adversity or not (Dryden, 2019a). By believing that you cannot tolerate the adversity, you are markedly reducing your ability to tolerate it even if you choose to do so, in the spirit of self-defeatism and self-fulfilling prophesy. Non-tolerance reduces one's behavioural repertoire down to avoidance, escape, and attack. Tolerance makes possible engagement, assessment, assertive approach, but also leaves the door open to avoidance and escape if necessary.

FT and the pursuit of excellence

Developing FT believes is important amidst the myriad pain, discomfort, rejection, and failure they face as ubiquitous features of a meaningful life pursuit. Believing that you can tolerate these adversities, while rationally recognizing that they are indeed very tough to tolerate and as a fallible human being you may experience suffering, is a useful, perhaps indispensable, form of barrier self-efficacy (Bandura, 1997). As Michael Jordan (basketball legend) famously said: "Obstacles don't have to stop you. If you run into a wall, don't turn around and give up. Figure out how to climb it, go through it, or work around it". This example from Jordan speak to a commitment and willingness to tolerate certain difficulty and discomfort, and underline the importance of helping clients to aim for meaningful goals. Taking on the pursuit of a truly meaningful goal will often necessitate the tolerance of much adversity, making tolerance of difficulty and discomfort worthwhile and infused with meaning. The fulfilment of potential is only achieved through tolerance of difficulty and discomfort; that is in part how we know our goals are meaningful. So not only is FT expressed through articulated beliefs ("it is tough, but I can bear it"), it is also expressed through voluntarily taking on difficult and demanding tasks that could bring about negative emotions. Helping a client to learn that they can stand discomfort can help them face adversities more easily, take greater risks, and work harder to maximize their productivity (DiGiuseppe et al., 2014). Marcus Aurelius intimates this ethos by stating "If it's endurable, then endure it. Stop complaining".

Stretching FT

Finally, how about issuing a challenge to the clients we work with to stretch their FT beliefs? Perhaps we can ask clients, "just how much can you tolerate?", "if you worked at it, and really focussed your energy on it, how much tolerance could you develop?", or "why don't we try to find out just how much you can tolerate, before we assume what you can or cannot tolerate?" I bet that you can tolerate more than you think you can. This is not to say that we should encourage clients to throw themselves into dangerous situations or stoically (small "s") enter into brutal environments just to test and develop their tolerance. But it does mean that we can encourage clients to take on reasonable challenges that start to push the boundaries of their tolerance. In other words, this is not a call to accept or encourage client burnout, but is a suggestion to enable clients to take on the heaviest weight they *can* carry, and work on *bearing* it, making use of the value placed in a meaningful and sustaining goal. The goal has to be sufficient and worthwhile enough to sustain them and fortify them against the inevitable suffering experienced in pursuit of that goal. This does not mean sacrifice everything in the name of hedonistic glory, as it could be that the biggest load you can carry is raising a family, doing good in your community, lifting those around you out of destitution. Tolerance can be heightened incrementally by pushing yourself, then resting, pushing yourself, resting. It's like Gareth Southgate (Manager of the England Men's Soccer Team) said when he spoke about his famous penalty miss in the 1996 European Championships: "I've learnt a million things from the day and the years that have followed it . . . the biggest thing being that when something goes wrong in your life, it doesn't finish you" (Wallace, 2018).

Awfulizing versus Anti-Awfulizing

Awfulizing; a belief that the adversity is *so* bad, that it couldn't be any worse (Dryden, 2019a). For a person holding awfulizing beliefs, the adversity is the worst thing they can imagine. For example, a client might believe that "it would be absolutely awful if I was not selected for this job" or "it would be completely terrible if my colleagues rejected me". In contrast, anti-awfulizing beliefs are when a person believes that the adversity is bad (perhaps very bad), but it is *not* awful, it is *not* the worst thing they can imagine (Dryden, 2019a). For example, a client might believe that "it would be bad if I was not selected for this job, but certainly not awful" or "it would be inconvenient if my colleagues rejected me, but not terrible". A good example of anti-awfulizing comes from Jurgen Klopp after failing to win in his first three matches in charge of Liverpool Football Club (Agence France-Presse, 2015). Klopp states:

> This is not the end of the world. We conceded a goal near the end, and it felt like the end of the world, but it is not the end of the world . . . I hope I'm not the only person in the stadium who thought: "This is not the end of the world". We can work on this . . . Of course, it is not the best moment for us, because we wasted a lot of energy. Southampton haven't lost away from home, so we had to work hard . . . You score the goal and you want to win, but it didn't happen for us today. Football is not a fairytale. Sometimes we can write stories like this but it doesn't always happen.

Awfulizing is not to be confused with "catastrophizing" because in REBT awfulizing is an irrational belief while catastrophizing is a cognitive consequence (Dryden, 2012a). Awfulizing reflects the irrational belief that nothing could be worse, the event in question is 100% bad or worse, no good could possibly come from this bad event, and this event cannot be transcended or surmounted – the event is awful, terrible, the end of the world (Dryden, 2019a). Awfulizing is about "believing that unpleasant or negative events are the worst they could conceivably be" (Dryden & Neenan, 1995, p. 9). In contrast, catastrophizing is a distorted cognitive consequence that reflects "a tendency to over-estimate a perceived threat and the corresponding seriousness of its impact" (Waltman & Palermo, 2019, p. 44). It is more reflective of over-estimating the likelihood that something bad will happen, over-estimating how bad it will be or is, and underestimating one's ability to cope with it (Craske et al., 2014; Gellatly & Beck, 2016). In other words, awfulizing is more extreme than catastrophizing.

Awfulizing is irrational because it is extreme - it does not allow for the fact that there are things that *could* be worse than the current adversity. Awfulizing is also inconsistent with reality because we cannot prove that the adversity is awful – we can prove that the adversity is bad, it might be very *very* bad (e.g., it might tangibly impede a goal), but we cannot prove that it is more than 100% bad. Just because something is really *really* bad, does not mean that it is awful (Dryden & Branch, 2008). Anti-awfulizing should not be thought of as casually minimizing the badness of a very negative event (e.g., "it's not that bad!"), rather, it shows that nothing is truly awful in the universe (Dryden & Branch, 2008). Importantly, the practitioner and client need to be on exactly the same page when it comes to semantics surrounding awfulizing. What does the client mean by "awful" or "terrible"? Do they mean "nothing could be worse", or do they mean "very very bad"? If it is the later, then the client might not be awfulizing, but they could be catastrophizing. In helping clients to articulate awfulizing, to aid clarity it is useful to have them include the recognition that the event is *beyond* bad, prior to asserting its awfulness (e.g., "the situation is not just bad, it is awful").

Where is your belief getting you?

For many people, the distinction between awfulizing and anti-awfulizing is academic and pointless, especially when they are experiencing emotional disturbance. Let's take for example a client who becomes injured and is told that their sport career is over by the team doctor, due to the injury. While the client would understandably evaluate the adversity as really bad, and averse to their goal of fulfilling their potential, they may also apply an extreme awfulizing evaluation to the adversity, taking it from "really bad" to "awful", "terrible", where "nothing could be worse". But of course, it *could* be worse (e.g., they are still alive!), and thus the adversity is not truly "awful". However, this is where the practitioner applies empathy and tact. There is little benefit here in disputing the awfulness of the adversity while the client is in the midst of undoubted turmoil, where one could *understandably* describe the adversity as "awful". Trying to convince the client that the adversity is not as bad as they think it is, or not as bad as it possibly could be, is a less than helpful strategy in this situation (DiGiuseppe et al., 2014). The misconstrued and assumed mistreatment of awfulizing beliefs has bolstered some of the misplaced criticisms of REBT – callously telling clients that what they have experienced is "technically not truly awful" under the protection of a "it's not the event but your beliefs that it is awful that is causing your emotions" world view. We do not do this in REBT. The REBT practitioner wants more than anything to help the client through difficult times, so would not kick a client when they are down (or at all!), risking the destruction of the therapeutic alliance and also damaging the client's chances of moving on functionally from the adversity.

In cases like the above career ending injury, the current author favours helping the client to think about the function or utility of their awfulizing belief, rather than the evidence and logic behind it (e.g., DiGiuseppe et al., 2014). The practitioner can validate the client's belief that the adversity is very bad, and ask them to consider whether believing that the adversity is awful is helpful for them to healthily move forward with their life at this time. We can encourage the client to consider whether they can adopt a more helpful belief that might serve them better as they begin to move forward after the tragic event. Then, as time passes, we can address the truth and logic of the awfulizing belief – ensuring the full disputation of the irrational belief – with a view to helping the client a) to move on from the event functionally, but also b) to fortify them against future hardship. The practitioner does this to help reduce the UNE, even though at times these conversations can be tough for both client and practitioner. However, just because the client holds awfulizing beliefs about the adversity now, it does not mean they will continue to hold awfulizing beliefs over time (Dryden, 2019b). Time-limited irrationality (Neenan & Dryden, 2015) does not necessarily need to be targeted for change, unless it persists, and the client can't get out of believing this way. Another strategy is to work with other core beliefs surrounding the adversity. DiGiuseppe et al. (2014) suggest that clients who experience a severe adversity often hold FI and demandingness beliefs in addition to awfulizing. The practitioner can more tactfully help the client to understand that they are strong enough to bear the significant adversity they have faced, and that if they do so, they might be able to glean some important meaning from it.

It is best to target awfulizing when the client is clearly applying awfulizing beliefs to adversities that would not be considered truly awful ("the worst thing that could possibly happen") by the vast majority of people. In other words, social consensus would *not* validate and confirm the client's use of "terrible" and "awful" in relation to the adversity. Empirically, nothing that *actually* happens, can be as bad what *could* possibly happen. It can always be worse; thus we never max out the potential awfulness of life. Thus, what happens to people in their lives are never awful by comparison with what *could* happen. Human beings have both the gift and the curse of being able to conjure up adversity in our minds, seeing and feeling future potential adversity, and the badness of that adversity is constrained only by the limits of our imagination. So, when working with a client who is applying awfulizing to being sacked, underperforming, being disrespected by others, for example, we can confidently apply disputation to the awfulizing, but still tread carefully. When doing this, we are not downplaying or undermining the adversity, we are just helping the client to avoid evaluating that adversity in an extreme and distorted manner.

I end this section with a brief snippet of a conversation between comedian Dave Chappelle and late-night talk show host David Letterman (Late Show, 2017). In the conversation, Chappelle puts failure into perspective, and reveals how this perspective helps him take chances:

Chappelle: Oh my god you're a comedian, well what happens if you go out there, and you tell your jokes, and no one laughs? . . . nothing happens. . . . You get paid the same, you're not gonna die, nothing bad happens. So I keep it all in perspective.

Letterman: Well, good for you, to keep it in perspective, because its something that I was never able to keep in perspective.

Chappelle: but I'm of the belief that the best comedians bomb hard, when they bomb, they bomb hard, you take chances, sometimes you fall flat sometimes you do great.

Depreciation (Global Evaluation) versus Unconditional Acceptance

Depreciation beliefs are where a person gives themselves, others, or the world, a global negative evaluation (Dryden, 2019a). They evaluate a specific trait, behaviour, or action, according to a standard of desirability or worth, which is plausible, but then *implausibly* apply the evaluation to their entire being (MacInnes, 2004). For example, a client might believe that "if I fail to reach my goals, that means I am complete failure" or "if my colleagues treats me badly, that means they are completely bad and rotten people". In other words, not only have I failed, I am a failure.

Not only did they treat me badly, they are completely bad people for doing so. In contrast, unconditional acceptance beliefs are where a person acknowledges that they, others, and the world, are too complex to merit a global evaluation (Dryden, 2019a). They recognize and understand that although people do bad or stupid things, they cannot be globally rated as bad or stupid, and that the world is full of normal fallible, imperfect human beings (including them!) who will make mistakes (e.g., Szentagotai & Jones, 2010). For example, a client might believe that "failing to reach my goal does not make me a complete failure, because my achievements do not define me as a human being" or "my colleagues treating me badly does not make them completely bad people, they are just normal fallible human beings just like everyone else". With acceptance beliefs, it is important that the client supplement their evaluation that the adversity is "bad" or "not ideal" with the negation of depreciation ("but that does not make me a failure") and an assertion of acceptance ("I am a fallible human being whether I succeed or not") (Dryden, 2009b).

Acceptance in REBT does not mean resignation to the situation. Condonement is not a requisite of acceptance – we can accept that hunger, poverty, war, suffering, exists in our world without condoning these things. Indeed, by accepting that these things are real it actually can enable us to do something about them (CCBT, 2021). We don't have to like something just because we accept it. Despite our limitations, and amidst the trials and tribulations that befell our ancestors to get us to this point in existence, it is perhaps more appropriate to be grateful for our existence than place any value on the self. There is much about life and the human species that is not perfect, but the capacity to evaluate aspects of our lives evidences our sentient humanness, a fallible aliveness that should call forth our humility and gratitude.

So, depreciation and unconditional acceptance really have two parts to them. Depreciation has the global evaluation piece but also the contingent self-worth piece as an underlying feature. For depreciation, it is my position that my value is contingent upon how I perform that provides the basis for my global evaluation that "because I have failed, that means I am a complete failure". For unconditional acceptance, it is my position that my value is in no way contingent upon how I perform that provides the basis for my acceptance that "just because I have failed does not mean I am a complete failure, and I am a fallible human being whether I succeed or not".

Human worth

> *I never really enjoyed the games. There was too much at stake playing for United. I always struggled in the periods I was out the team or playing badly. I had a feeling of worthlessness. As a footballer you wonder if your team-mates are looking at you and asking the questions you are asking of yourself. Why can't he hit a decent pass? Why's he always injured? What's wrong with him?*
>
> –Ryan Giggs (Manchester United FC and Wales soccer player)

In REBT, human beings are neither valuable nor invaluable – the question of value is inappropriate with regards to a human being (or any being). Ellis (1996c) communicated two main positions on human value. In one view, Ellis tells us that believing "I am good because I exist" is a tautological, unprovable, and un-disprovable supposition, and is in the same class with the statement, "I am bad because I exist". Ellis says

> I do not have intrinsic worth or worthlessness, but merely aliveness. I'd better rate my traits and acts but not my totality or "self". I fully accept myself, in the sense that I know I have aliveness, and I choose to survive and live as happily as possible, and with minimum needless pain. I only require this knowledge and this choice – and no other kind of self-rating.
>
> (p. 5)

He does however, also recognize the affective utility in assuming that you have intrinsic value because you are alive rather than assuming that you have no value. But Ellis (1996c) reinforces that "philosophically, it remains an untenable proposition" (p. 5). So, the global evaluation of one's worth as a person is always irrational, because there is no agreed upon standard or science or logic to human rating (Ruggiero et al., 2018). In sum, we can rate acts, deeds, and traits in light of our goals, but we cannot rate our self, being, or totality (Ellis, 1983).

Acceptance is important, but let us not forget the "unconditionality" of this acceptance. This is vital because it suggests your human worth is not conditional on what you do (or do not do). Rather, there is nothing you can do to increase or decrease your human worth. There is no evidence that you have any intrinsic and inherent worth or value as a human being, and thus, you are not more valuable because you succeed, and you are not less valuable because you fail. Attaching worth to human beings is non-sensical because of the immutability of our humanness, complexity, uniqueness, fallibility, and changeability. Many high performers recognize that there is a danger in conflating self-worth with behaviour. For example, Lizzie Simmonds (GB Olympic swimmer) states that "I developed a self-limiting belief that my worth as a person was correlated to my performance in the pool". Allied to this, Ellis (1991) notes that "Almost the entire history of Western civilization has been motivated by the dubious proposition that human beings are worthwhile only when they are extrinsically competent, successful, or achieving" (p. 147).

So, REBT has a unique position on human-worth (Dryden, 2019a), underpinned by the notions that humans are human until we die (humanness), that humans are too complex for a single global rating (complexity), that each human is unique (uniqueness), that all humans make mistakes (fallibility), and that humans are constantly in flux (changeability). Thus, depreciation beliefs are irrational in part because they fail to endorse these positions on human worth. But depreciation is also irrational because it is dysfunctional, in that the tendency to make global evaluations, while facilitating rapid judgements about the world, is error prone because it reflects global, stable, and definitive conclusions based on low-frequency behaviours or events (Szentagotai & Jones, 2010). Indeed, "the whole is more than the sum of its parts" (Aristotle, from Metaphysica, tr. 1963). To evaluate the whole based on its parts reflects inaccurate overgeneralizing. Evaluate the action/s, not the actor.

In all, a client who believes that their worth or value as a human being can be inflated or deflated on the basis of their achievements, is potentially on the road to nowhere, and the practitioner should help them work towards unconditional self-acceptance. There are some really good examples of high achieving people separating the person from the behaviour. For example, Ellie Robinson, MBE (English swimmer, multi world record holder) states that "I went through a phase where I thought that only medals would define me or if I didn't have a medal, then I was no-one . . . you don't need medals to be someone . . . I am so much more than my medals" (Channel 4 Paralympics, 2021).

I am what I do

There is a tendency, when the stakes are high and the situation is important to us, to wrap our self-worth up with the results of our endeavours. Also, for clients who develop a strong work identity, depreciation might be particularly salient and dangerous. Naomi Osaka (professional tennis player, two-time Grand Slam winner) said that "It was become a champion, or probably be broke. . . . For so long I've tied winning to my worth as a person. To anyone that would know me, they know me for being a tennis player. So, like, what am I if I'm not a good tennis player?" In sport, athletic identity is the degree of strength and exclusivity to which an individual identifies with the athlete role (Brewer et al., 1991), and a person with high athletic identity is more likely to interpret an event in terms of its implications for their athletic functioning (Sparkes, 1998). The notion of exclusivity in athletic identify represents the extent to which an individual's identity and self-worth are determined solely by their athletic performance (Brewer & Cornelius, 2001). A strong exclusive athletic identity could abet emotional disturbance in light of deselection, injury, and retirement, for example (e.g., Brewer et al, 1993; Edison et al., 2021), and athletes are more likely to ruminate and catastrophize in adverse times (Costa et al., 2020). Indeed, recent research indicated that stronger endorsement of irrational beliefs is related to higher athletic identity (Michel-Kröhler & Turner, 2022). But in contrast, athletic identity could contribute to an emotional connection to sport and have beneficial effects on involvement in physical activity and athletic performance (Babić et al., 2015). It is of course not only athletes who can develop a strong identity oriented around their vocation, but all of us are in danger of doing this in our work pursuits, an idea recognized many years ago by Al Petitpas (1978), amongst others.

There are consistencies between defining the self on the basis of a vocational pursuit, and the notion of depreciation or global evaluation, such that those who exclusively see themselves as a "teacher", "athlete", "soldier" (these are just examples of vocational roles) who then fail, are more likely to consider *themselves* as complete failures. So if your total self is fused with your vocational pursuit, such that your work self is the totality of the self, then it is more likely that failure will be met with depreciation. This is important because as a human being, you will fail. A lot (!). If I completely define myself in line with my work pursuits ("I am a doctor, that is everything I am"), and hold depreciation beliefs ("I am a failure if I fail), within a context of ubiquitous and inevitable adversity (i.e., failure), then I am in precarious position with regards to my well-being (Turner et al., 2022a). Seemingly as an antidote to athletic identity and depreciation, Ben Foster (Watford and England goal keeper) in an interview with The Guardian (Fisher, 2020) spoke about his breadth of interests and his reluctance to label himself as "a footballer":

> If you ask me who I am, I would say: "I'm a father, a husband, I love cycling, I play football for a living, blah, blah, blah"... but the problem comes when straightaway people say: "I'm a professional footballer". Come on, mate. You're not – you're a human being first. But that comes with age. And that's the thing you need to get into people's heads, that they are people first. People see them as this commodity, this footballer, but they are a person first and foremost.

Allied to this, Ellis (2005b) states that "Your performance is part of you, but certainly not all of you".

A critical point about apathy

One (misplaced) criticism of REBT could be that in unconditional acceptance there is the possibility of stagnation and reluctance to change, or even apathy. If I unconditionally accept myself, then why change? Why try to improve? Why not just accept who I am, and stay the same? This is a confusion between self versus role, traits, or behaviours. The focus should be on the improvement of goal-related behaviours (goal as in "Goals; FG and PG", not just performance related targets). In other words, we are not suggesting that clients accept being a "bad boss", or an "inattentive spouse", or a "low skilled athlete". Unconditional acceptance is not a proxy for self-efficacy, and clients can still identify *aspects* of themselves that they do not accept, and thus want to develop competencies within. "I accept myself" is not the same as "I am contented with everything about myself". We can help clients become more skilled, more attentive, more empathetic, etc., because behaviours can be rated, evaluated, and of course can be changed, and we can measure this change. Importantly though, as these behaviours improve, this positive shift does not make the client more worthwhile, or more valuable as a human being.

A final word on beliefs

In this chapter I have outlined what beliefs are in REBT and have defined each of the rational and irrational beliefs. But when is a belief not a belief, and should we take all irrational utterances seriously? If a client has a fleeting thought that "I am such a massive loser" but does not take this seriously, by which I mean to say, does not give this belief credence, then it is highly likely that the thought will not be problematic for the client. *Not all irrational utterances or thoughts are suitable targets for change*. Indeed, Dryden and Neenan (2020) talk about time-limited irrationalities, whereby despite having an irrational thought, some clients may be able to stand back and cope with the adversity, and thus do not consider the irrationality to be a problem. They also state that some clients do disturb themselves about an event but are able to engage in rationality fairly quickly. So, many people can apply irrational beliefs to their adversities and suffer acutely, but then return to a "normal" (undisturbed) state quite quickly, realizing their irrationality and addressing it. But if suffering continues and irrationality contributes to perpetual unhealthy emotion, and or the client is stuck with their irrational beliefs (Dryden & Neenan, 2020), then we can target irrationality for intervention. Not all irrationality will underpin disturbance, and all disturbance is not underpinned by irrationality.

Thus, as practitioners it is important that we do not "jump on" every "irrational" utterance within hearing distance – we are not the rationality police. On this issue, Robb and Ciarrochi (2005) suggest that "trouble comes when certain kinds of private, or public, language is not only prevalent but also "believed" (p. 170). They suggest that when we "believe" something, it means that we "take it seriously" such that the belief in some way determines our behaviour. This goes beyond mere utterances that seem to have a flavour of irrationality. Does the client really believe what they are saying or thinking? If not, then their irrationality could be just a cathartic expression of their frustration ("you idiot! What a terrible shot!"), for example. However, if the client does really believe what are saying or thinking, then their irrationality might be a true and accurate reflection of a deeply held and potentially pernicious philosophy that they hold on to and which helps determine their emotional and behavioural reactivity to adverse events.

Therefore, perhaps the issue lays not within the demand for fair treatment, for example, but in my conviction in the belief that I must be treated fairly. The more strongly I believe that I must be treated fairly, the more likely I am to evince dysfunctional emotions and behaviours. The thought "I must be treated fairly" may appear in my mind's eye fleetingly, and I do not take it seriously. But if I do take it seriously, then I risk problematic consequences. The level of belief in a dysfunctional cognition may influence the level of consequent dysfunction (e.g., Beck, 2015). Indeed, Beck and Freeman (1990) note that it is the intensity to which a dysfunctional belief is held that influences the level of dysfunction it will promote. Collard (2022) also points out that if a person views a dysfunctional cognition as just a spurious and fleeting event, it would be less likely to drive dysfunction. For example, an irrational, potentially depreciating, thought like "I am such an idiot" could be held lightly and humorously, not held tightly or truthfully, and thus would not be pathological. In REBT, we encourage clients to not take seriously, and actively work against, beliefs that are irrational, and to take seriously and actively strengthen, beliefs that are rational.

Summary

This chapter is a bit weighty, but I make no apologies, because beliefs are at the centre of REBT and as such need to be fully articulated and understood (by us, and our clients). In the current chapter I have tried to communicate the nature of beliefs in REBT, including the background for rationality as codified by Ellis. If we are to develop and express (or apply) our rationality, we must work over a lifetime to think and act against irrationality, and think and act in congruence with rationality. It is not accurate to categorize human beings as rational or irrational, rather, in line with REBT, we can think and act in rational ways, and we can think and act in irrational ways, but these thoughts and actions do not define us. In response to adversity and stressors, human beings are rather adept at thinking and acting in ways that makes things worse. In REBT, we help clients to *not make things worse* first of all, and then we can help them to *make things better*. REBT is designed to help people live longer, minimize their self-defeating proclivities and suffering, but also to "actualize themselves so as to live a more fulfilling and happier existence" (DiGiuseppe et al., 2014, p. 14).

I finish this chapter with a segment of a speech delivered by Brandon Brooks, who at the time of speaking was American football guard for the Philadelphia Eagles of the National Football League. He was speaking at his commencement speech at Miami University. For me, this captures nicely some of the content of this chapter from an athlete's perspective. He says:

> I took being the best very seriously, too seriously in fact. I *demanded excellence* of myself, I *demanded perfection*, no mistakes, no screwups. I wanted to epitomise perfection. I did not want to make mistakes, until I did, and when that did happen, the world wasn't a good place for me . . . I don't know how many of you know but I have anxiety disorder. I *demanded perfection* of myself and when I failed, when I'm not the superhuman I'm supposed to be, my body and my mind turned on me, where I get tremendously ill for hours and can't play the sport I love. I missed 5 NFL games over my career because I couldn't handle not being perfect. I came to a crossroads where I had to make a decision. I would either cave under the pressure, or get help, persevere and rise to the occasion. I choose the latter because there are no diamonds without pressure . . . Of all the accomplishments I've had this year, Pro Bowl, Superbowl, I am especially proud of defeating the anxiety that has affected me in the past. I learned through therapy to not worry or care about making a mistake. Why? *Because the best thing about life is, it goes on.* How many times have you thought the worst situation, and *how often has that worst scenario ever came to fruition? Rarely. We're all allowed to make mistakes, to be imperfect, to be human.* Learn that now, listen to someone who knows, learn from your mistakes, keep pushing, trust yourself, and trust the process.

8 Assessing beliefs (B)

Now we know the particulars of the rational and irrational beliefs, we know what we are looking for. So, we can help the client to uncover their irrational beliefs. I say uncover, because sometimes beliefs are not just sitting on the surface of our awareness waiting to be happened upon and challenged. It seems to me that irrational beliefs lay dormant until we experience (i.e., appraise) a situation that is incongruent with an important goal (i.e., G-A incongruence). Speaking to the depth with which irrational beliefs are held, Albert Ellis states that "People's basic self-disturbing musts and demands are not merely superficially or consciously held, but are often tacit, implicit, and unconscious and are strongly clung to in the "deep" structures of their minds and bodies" (Ellis, 2014, in DiGiuseppe et al., 2014). When we face adversity, the irrational belief becomes salient in influencing emotional and behavioural reactivity, and at that point might be experienced as a declarative and explicit thought. The belief simply isn't relevant to us until we face A, or our Gs are threatened. Beliefs in REBT tend to be *about* A and or *about* G, and I argue, are triggered by A representing an event (internal or external) that is incongruent with G. As such, if we want to help clients to access these deeper beliefs, we need to become skilled in bringing these beliefs to the surface – I discuss strategies for this goal in this chapter.

For many of the clients I have worked with, they have held their irrational beliefs for as long as they can remember. This means that they are often not acutely aware of these beliefs, and when they become aware (in our sessions) they are sometimes reticent to question and abandon these beliefs – and so they should be! We should not expect people to so quickly abandon their beliefs. In contrast, I have worked with many clients who do have very good access to their beliefs and seem to be able to articulate and critically analyse them with very little introspection. In other words, don't assume either is the case, and be prepared for both scenarios, and work on a case-by-case basis.

Asking the right questions

Because revealing irrational beliefs at least to some extent requires introspection, when we are helping clients to identify their irrational beliefs, we help them go beyond A. Inference chaining, covered earlier in this book, can help with this and

DOI: 10.4324/9781003508472-9

is my preferred method for revealing, or getting close to, B. But there are other strategies we can employ. When we ask, "what were you thinking when that event occurred?" or "what thoughts were you aware of when in that situation?" we could get answers that reflect inferences at A. Therefore, we can encourage the client to think more deeply by asking questions like, "What were you telling yourself about A (client's critical A) that made you feel C (client's UNE)?" In other words, we are helping the client to understand that a) the A is not causing C, b) that there is something they have probably not told us that is important, and c) that it is whatever they were telling themselves *about A* that helped to cause C. There are variations of this enquiry, such as, "what are you telling yourself about the critical A that is leading to C?" or "is there anything you are thinking *about* A that might be *causing* C?" Don't expect a quick answer on this. Some will come straight back to you with an irrational belief (or the echoes of one), some will take a while to ask the question to themselves and let it percolate in their mind a little. If they are struggling, then try some variations of the question.

Another technique, that relates to the questioning above, that I find useful is to present a graphical representation of the ABC aspects of the GABCDE framework and help the client to input their As and Cs into the A and C boxes (as it were). Then they can see that there is something missing in the B box. As you pose the question using this illustration to help the client understand, and perhaps discover and report, this missing link by attempting to introspect on their more deeply held beliefs. This also serves as a nice record of the ABCs that the client can take with them to reflect upon, perhaps tweak, and build upon.

All these questions, including questioning used in inference chaining, are examples of Socratic dialogue which is very useful to encourage self-discovery. Using these approaches, you can help the client to reveal and articulate their irrational beliefs perhaps for the first time, which can trigger a "light bulb moment" for them, in which they vocalize what has not been vocalized for perhaps a very long time (or ever). It can be a powerful moment, that you can capitalize on by making sure the belief is fully articulated. That is, don't settle for "it is awful to not be approved of", instead, try to encourage the expression of the full preference-demand-awfulizing irrational belief (e.g., "I want to be, and therefore I must be, approved of and it would be awful if I was not") by enquiring further upon what they might be telling themselves about the A (or G of course).

Hypothesizing

We can also be more forthright and share some hypotheses about the beliefs with the client. DiGiuseppe et al. (2014) call this "Deductive Hypotheses Driven Assessment" (p. 140). I mentioned earlier in the book that the relationship that the practitioner has with the client can be characterized as "scientists in cahoots" and the notion of formulating hypotheses is in line with this characterization. The practitioner generates these hypotheses based on their experience and knowledge of REBT (and psychotherapy/applied psychology per se), the client (and people in general), and psychology/psychopathology. Once you have generated a hypothesis, you can share this with the client, but the hypothesis needs to be carefully considered and carefully presented to the client.

When presenting the hypothesis to the client, do so in an inquisitive and genuine manner, expressing your desire and intent to help the client to figure out what they could be telling themselves about A that is leading to C. This is not a "this is what you are telling yourself, aren't you?" because this is too leading and authoritative. There is no point putting words in the client's mouth because it is *their* beliefs you are trying to locate and work with, not yours. I first formally learned about this technique while studying in New York at the Albert Ellis Institute, and thus follow DiGiuseppe et al.'s (2014) guidance:

1. Use suppositional language, such as "could it be that you are not only believing that being disrespected is *tough*, but that it is also *intolerable*?" Or "do you think that it is possible that performing well is not just preferable to you, but that you *must* perform well?" Or "when you were in that situation, is there a chance that you were thinking that it was terrible or awful, or something like that?"
2. Avoid declarative statements. Try not to say "I don't think you are just saying X to yourself, I think you are actually saying Y". Most clients do not like to be told what they are thinking.
3. Drop the ego. Remember, you and the client are scientists in cahoots, you are not a Sage or a Guru. Your suggestions might be false, so take an open and non-defensive stance when you present your hypotheses.
4. Seek client feedback. When you present your hypotheses, you are doing so in the form of a question in order to elicit feedback from the client. Whether you are correct, close to correct, or completely incorrect, is decided by the client. This can be in the form of verbal feedback, which is ideal, but can also come in non-verbal forms. Be attentive to body language, tone of voice, eye movement, and any signal that might allude to emotionality. You can quite often tell when you have presented something that the client connects with by observing their reactions to it. You can then reflect this back to the client, for example, "I noticed that when I made that suggestion to you, you grew fidgety in your chair. Why might that be?"

Why would you want to use a Deductive Hypotheses Driven Assessment? Well, say you have a client who, after various methods of Socratic dialogue, is not quite able to identify and or articulate the belief. It might be on their tip of their tongue; they may be skirting around the edge of the belief. Shall we just let them hang there until they happen upon the belief? Or do we make some well-informed suggestions that could push them over the edge? We have all experienced a situation in which somebody said something in such a way that made us think "that's exactly what I believe, but I didn't know I believed it before they just said it". This is what great literature or art stirs up within us, and it sometimes requires an outside perspective to help us realize what we believe. Also, what's the worst that can happen? So long as you have developed a good working alliance with the client, and you have prepared them well for this kind of interaction, then there is little harm in presenting hypotheses to the client with a view to helping them. I have never had a situation where my hypotheses have led to working alliance rupture, but this could happen if the practitioner does not follow the guidance proposed in the four points above. Self-discovery is powerful and should be striven for as the first port of call, but how long are we willing to wait for this self-discovery? In keeping with the brief way in which REBT can be applied, I argue that we should prioritize and create opportunities for self-discovery, but not be afraid of suggestion in the form of collaborative hypothesis venturing and testing. An articulated self-discovered realization (inside-out) has the benefit of authenticity and ownership for the client, but it is still very powerful when a deeply held belief is revealed to the client from outside-in (i.e., by the practitioner).

Choice

Dryden also developed a technique called the "Choice-Based Assessment of IBs" (DiGiuseppe et al., 2014) which in my experience is very effective. In this assessment, the practitioner:

(1) Asserts the client's preference about A and elicits the client's agreement (e.g., "So it is important for you to be respected by the manager, is that right?")
(2) State that the client could hold one of two beliefs that account for the UNE (unhealthy anger) at C and ask for permission to present them to the client (e.g., "Would it be ok if I suggested two beliefs that you could have been holding at the time you were angry? Can I outline them and then you can tell me which belief, if any, related to your anger?")
(3) State the client's C and then present the two beliefs; one demand belief, one preference belief (e.g., "At the time when you were angry, was your anger based on a belief that 'It's preferable to be respected by the manager, and therefore I must be', or is it more of a belief that 'It's preferable to be respected by the manager, but that does not mean that I must be?'"
(4) Ask the client which belief they think may have accounted for their UNE (anger).

The Dubois method

One method, that is inspired by Paul Dubois, and shares some characteristics with Dryden's choice-based approach above, encourages the client to consider that they are building a second, and third, story about A. Dubois suggested, "do not add phobophobia to the phobia that torments you, that would be building a second story to your malady" (Dubois, 1905, p. 367) and "Do not let us build a second story to our sorrow by being sorry for our sorrow" (Dubois, 1909, p. 236). So, we might say to the client:

> Oftentimes we tell ourselves a story in our minds about what happens to us, and this story can be accurate, or it can be inaccurate, and we can take it at

face value. But sometimes, we then tell ourselves a second story about that first story, and then we can tell ourselves a third story about the second story, which is often quite unhelpful. In the first story we can say "my boss ignored me", in the second story we can say "and that's a bad thing", and in the third story we can say "but it's not the end of the world, I can certainly tolerate it" or we can say "and it's terrible to be treated this way and I cannot bear it!" So, when you consider the situation you have described, what are the second and third stories you are telling yourself?

This tri-story idea is also captured by Ellis (1994) when he refers to cold, warm, and hot cognitions, whereby negative warm cognitions generate negative emotions, and rigid and extreme hot cognitions underpin emotional disturbance. In the above example the cold cognition ("my boss ignored me"), warm cognition ("that's a bad thing"), and hot cognition ("it's terrible, and I cannot bear it!") could underpin unhealthy anger, for example. We can help the client to understand these story layers, and that it is the specific hot cognitions, or third stories, that are most problematic, and we can then help the client to identify their third stories (i.e., irrational beliefs).

Triggering B

Another useful method that we can use to extrapolate the B is to guide the client in the use of imagery. Here, the practitioner asks the client to close their eyes, get relaxed, and imagine in their mind's eye the situation (A) in which they felt the UNE (e.g., unhealthy anger). You can observe body language for signs of engagement and affect to get a sense for whether the client is successful in stirring up the emotion imaginally. Once the client is deeply within this image, ask the client to recall what was going through their mind in that situation. As the event unfolded, what were they telling themselves about the event that was adding fuel to the emotional fire? Some clients might not possess the requisite imagery ability for this activity, so we may need to teach them how to image, or we could apply more sophisticated methods to recreate the situational stimuli (concrete and or inferred) in order to help access a problematic irrational belief. For example, virtual reality tools (e.g., Spence et al., 2019) can be used to enter clients into very realistic situations that mimic A, such as social-evaluative situations, in order to help trigger emotion reactivity. This can stimulate more deeply held beliefs because we are recreating (as far as we can) the conditions under which this belief is triggered.

In a similar vein, but non-virtually, we can expose the client to a situation that represents A, or gets close to A in terms of demand characteristics, in the session. In-session role play is useful for this purpose, where we enact the A in the room so as afford greater access to the beliefs shaping the emotion by triggering the beliefs and the emotion purposefully. Care is needed here not to distress the client, but an example might be the enactment of a difficult conversation the client is anxious about having with a significant other. The client acts as themselves, and the practitioner takes the place of the other party. The client then attempts the difficult conversation with the other party (the practitioner) so as to elicit the problematic emotions (albeit on a less intense level than would be evinced in the actual situation). This can bring the belief into the client's mind.

Lastly, with some forethought and organization, we can use video stimuli to trigger emotional reactivity (e.g., Zupan & Eskritt, 2020), ideally the emotion that the client is finding problematic. In reaction to selected emotionally provocative videos, we can encourage the client to report what they were thinking when viewing the videos. In sport and performance settings, it is often possible to go a step further and use actual performance footage of the client. Based on their felt emotion while watching the videos, we can enquire as to the inferences they are making and the beliefs they are applying to the video.

A downside of these triggering B techniques is that they mimic or get close to the A, but they are not the actual A and may not be accurate to the *critical* A. But they can get you into the ballpark in order to facilitate deeper conversations about G, A, and C, and could even stimulate B itself. What would be ideal is being in the actual adverse or activating event with the client in the "real world", which is more possible when working closely with organizations. But even if we are there in the moment, we still do not have access to the inferential aspects of A and as such do still need to engage the client in some dialogue about their experiences in order to access and assess B.

Questionnaires

The techniques described here can be used in conjunction and there is no "correct" or "best" method, as it depends on the client and the context. But taking shortcuts in assessing B is not advisable, since accurately identifying and then challenging B is crucial for specific REBT. To supplement the discursive assessment methods covered here, I also use various psychometrics to assess irrational beliefs. Clearly, psychometric questionnaires cannot access deeply held beliefs, but are useful for an indication of irrationality, or of a proclivity to endorse irrational beliefs, and as markers of client change as REBT is applied. The irrational performance beliefs inventory (Turner et al., 2018b) was developed for specific use in performance environments, such as work, military, sport, and exercise. Also, the Smarter Thinking Profile (smarterthinkingprofile.com; Turner & Wood, 2019b) offers a comprehensive assessment of irrational beliefs and can be completed by clients for free. This profile allows the client to download a report with details about their irrational beliefs across ten performance content areas (achievement, approval, consistency, development, failure, fairness, opportunity, rejection, respect, security). Also useful is the Attitudes and Belief Scale 2 (ABS-2; DiGiuseppe et al., 1988) which includes content areas of achievement, approval, comfort, justice, and control. Lastly, me and my team have developed the Rational and Irrational Ideas Inventory (RIII; Turner et al., 2026) which comprehensively assesses all rational and irrational core beliefs.

Is it a "belief"?

In unearthing irrational beliefs with clients, it is important to be aware that you will probably dig up many distorted cognitions and ideas that could be classified as irrational on the basis on an REBT definition. But before we take seriously these cognitive events and dispute them, we need to make sure that the client actual believes and endorses what they are reporting. Some thoughts are just fleeting irrationalities that are reflections of the many thoughts and ideas that pass through our minds, like shooting stars across the sky. Just because we hear irrationality (i.e., language that matches the four core irrational beliefs) this does not necessarily mean that the client believes or endorses this irrationality. In my experience, some clients (particularly young people) verbally project the irrationality that characterizes the climate in which they toil. In other words, they have been conditioned to regurgitate the irrational mantras expounded by key figures in their life – such as managers, teachers, parents, and friends. The client might parrot "it is terrible, intolerable, to fail" or "failing means you are a failure" because they have heard a significant person in their life say it, or because they believe it to be the "right thing to say". I do not blame clients for this – we all do this in some manner – often parroting political doctrines due to media brainwashing. So, it is important to address this with clients and try to go beyond what might just be a rehearsed rhetoric. When clients articulate irrationality, we can ask "do you really believe that?" and can even ask them to rate between 1–10 the extent to which they do truly believe it (1=do not believe, 10=totally believe). There is no sense in working with a belief that is not *really* endorsed. The same goes for rationality. A client may want to present themselves as rational, and thus might articulate rational beliefs. But if they do not really endorse this rationality, or do not really believe in that rational way, then we need to know so that we can increase their endorsement of this rationality.

What to do with B

In the next chapter I cover the disputation (D) of B. But what do we do in the immediate present when the client's B is revealed and articulated? In my practice, I write the irrational beliefs down on paper in front of the client, or a flipchart or whiteboard if one is available. There is evidence that thought suppression may paradoxically and counterproductively increase the frequency with which the targeted thought intrudes consciousness (e.g., Wegner et al., 1987; Rassin et al., 2000), and can increase acute autonomic nervous system activity and over time inhibition can serves as a cumulative stressor, increasing the probability of psychosomatic disease (Pennebaker & Susman, 1988). Further, expressing thoughts about an event, rather than suppressing these thoughts, can help with habituation (Roemer & Borkovec, 1994) and is associated with both immediate and long-term health benefit (Pennebaker, 1989). But these anti-suppression effects notwithstanding, I encourage the client to write their B down for five important reasons. First, it externalizes the B from within the client and is a commitment to articulating the belief accurately and fully. The focus of the session in that moment is not on the client themselves, but on the belief, which can be assuring for the client and is a less confrontational position to dispute from. Second, it facilitates distancing the client from the irrational beliefs (e.g., Collard, 2019; Hofmann et al., 2010) so that they, or we, can more openly apply a critical and analytical approach to the belief. The client is often less precious about the belief when it doesn't just exist in their own minds, but is out in the real world on paper. Third, it makes the irrational belief seem more real to have it presented in written form, and as such, the client views the belief as a more tangible phenomenon than if it was just a purely psychological event. The client can interact with the belief on paper in a way that they could not if it was just in their mind – then can rip it, throw it away, put a line through it, etc. Forth, the actual writing down of the belief leads to adjustment and refinement as together we figure out exactly how the belief is to be articulated. You may try various versions of the same belief to make sure that the wording is correct and accurate to what the client believes in their own language. Finally, the client can take this belief with them away from the session and work on challenging and disputing it, once we have done some disputation in the session. So, I recommend writing the belief down because this subtle approach to belief articulation can aid belief conceptualization, clarity, and disputation.

Summary

In this chapter I have covered ways in which the practitioner can assess B in order to help the client identify the irrational belief/s that is/are underpinning their UNE/s. These techniques are really designed for one main purpose, to help the client to become cognizant of philosophies, rules, and ideas that mediate the relationship between A and C. Some techniques reflect direct questions and postulations that are discussed with the client, while others are less direct. But the goal is the same: to clearly and unambiguously articulate the irrational beliefs that are underpinning the client's dysfunctional emotions and maladaptive behaviours. Next, we move onto addressing irrational beliefs, which in REBT, is known as Disputation (D).

9 Disputation (D)

"With practice, we can learn to monitor our thoughts and challenge the irrational ideas that cause unhealthy emotions and psychosomatic symptoms"

-Dubois (1906)

It is the challenging of irrational and rational beliefs that I tackle in this chapter. But before we enter the rough terrain of disputation, it is important to emphasize that only a rudimentary and unsophisticated REBT practitioner is obsessed with irrational beliefs and hellbent on disputation at all costs. Of course, an important aspect of specific REBT is the finding and disputing of irrational beliefs, and research evidence supports this approach (e.g., Jordana et al., 2023; King et al., 2024). This can only be meaningfully achieved with the commitment of the client to working on weakening their irrational beliefs and strengthening their rational beliefs. But a more sophisticated REBT practitioner recognizes that they need to help clients to also consciously take and profoundly imbibe a philosophy of acceptance (of the self, others, and the world) in several cognitive, emotional, and behavioural ways (Ellis, 2005a). Also, the REBT practitioner stresses a focus on goals and values, and pragmatically helps the client to work towards those goals and values (e.g., Ellis, 2005a). So, far from being an entirely remedial approach focussed on "fixing" faulty ideas, REBT is a proactive approach to helping clients fulfil their potential. With this important edification in mind, I now move on to exploring disputation in detail.

Disputation is a collaborative (client-practitioner) argument, or a debate, focussed on challenging the client's ideas, not the client themselves. As such, the practitioner should ensure that the client is ready for disputation. That is, it is a good idea to prepare the client for these challenges to their ideas, and make sure they understand what this will entail (Dryden & Branch, 2008). Part of the preparation for disputation is developing a strong working alliance which by now should be graced with good rapport, an agreed direction of travel for the work, and of course, a detailed idea of the Gs, As, Bs, and Cs. But in addition, it is advisable to explain to the client what disputation is, why it "needs" to take place, and how they can facilitate the process (i.e., "try to be inquisitive, open, and honest"). The client may have held and harnessed their irrational beliefs for

DOI: 10.4324/9781003508472-10

many years, and these axioms which have guided their lives may be deep rooted and entrenched; "people get unbelievably upset when you poke them in the axioms" (Peterson, 2017).

In disputation, what we do not want to do, and do not try to do, is help the client to develop meta-irrational beliefs. That is, do not encourage musts *about* musts (e.g., I must not demand fairness, I must not use the word "must"). Rather, we help the client to develop more flexible beliefs, such as preference and acceptance beliefs, rather than merely denigrating and judging irrational beliefs. In REBT, it is not the suppression of irrational beliefs that is the focus of the work, but the application of empirical, logical, and functional ideas to one's beliefs in service of greater human functioning. If we become too dogmatic about not holding irrational beliefs, we risk saddling the client with another problem, which is often presented as anger or guilt surrounding the holding of irrational beliefs.

Learning to dispute

> Knowledge or insight into one's irrational behavior only partially, if at all, helps one change it.
>
> -Ellis (1976, p. 33)

While the GABC elements of the framework have laid some vital groundwork for the REBT work, D is where the major intervention takes place (Turner & Barker, 2014). D is where the opportunity for real philosophic change can be instigated, and E (Effective New Belief; next chapter) is where this real change can be made habitual. A core rationale for undertaking disputation with the client, is that because the aetiology of irrational beliefs to some degree are natural (e.g., biological basis; Ellis, 1976; Ruth, 1992), and to some degree learned and rehearsed by the client probably over a long period of time (DiGiuseppe et al., 2014), then these beliefs need to be vigorously unlearned, and rational beliefs needs to be rehearsed instead so that they become habitual. Ultimately, society drives irrationality, and we as humans develop irrational beliefs as a function of our biological tendency to do so. So, clients are not usually going to give their irrational beliefs up willingly. Ellis (1976) believed not only that innate is the capacity to be irrational, but also innate is the difficulty in modifying or extinguish said irrationality (i.e., "modification-elimination difficulty"; Ruth, 1992, p. 6). Thus, helping clients to dispute, weaken, and abandon their irrational beliefs requires great effort and attention from client and practitioner.

Ellis recognized that "humans have a strong tendency to needlessly and severely disturb themselves, and that, to make matters much worse, they also are powerfully *predisposed* to unconsciously and habitually prolong their mental dysfunctioning and to fight like hell against giving it up" (Ellis, 1987b, p. 365). Ellis' core argument was that all humans at some point believe, think, and act in ways that are self-destructive, reflecting the illogicality of holding such beliefs, thoughts, and behaviours (Sharf, 1996). This is evident across all known social and cultural groups. He argues that all societal and cultural institutions promote demandingness, awfulizing, frustration intolerance, and depreciation to greater or lesser extents. Furthermore, irrational beliefs are exacerbated by those around us whom we look to for guidance on how to live our lives (Sharf, 1996). Even when society dissuades certain self-destructive behaviours, we are resistant to rationality and constantly think and act in ways that are contrary to the development of humanity. We give up many erroneous beliefs as we develop and mature, but irrational beliefs maintain.

So, disputation is often difficult because it is a complicated process in which the client confronts and challenges a long and tightly held belief on the basis of empirical fact, logical consistency, functional utility, and heuristic value, and then instantiates a new belief that is resilient to these scientific criteria (e.g., DiGiuseppe, 1986). We have to be mindful of the fact that not everybody can or will think critically about their thoughts and beliefs. We often take it for granted as psychologists or psychotherapists that people monitor their internal dialogue and assess its meaning and veracity, but scientific thinking is hard. That is in part why we have to *train* to be scientists. Even though it is the case that irrational beliefs are often stubbornly held, fortunately, "most people have considerable ability to think, to think about their thinking, and to think about thinking about their thinking . . . they can change" (Ellis, 1994, p. 138). This is evidenced in the corpus of literature that demonstrates that with REBT, irrational beliefs can be meaningfully reduced across a broad range of populations, with focussed one-to-one and group work (e.g., Jordana et al., 2023; King et al., 2024).

The importance of the client learning disputation properly also lays within the fact that in REBT disputation is not a remedial one-time deal. The client is specifically educated and trained in the principles of disputation so that they can execute disputation skills perpetually into the future across many events and emotions, and in the fact of many As. The client practices and rehearses this cognitive change strategy to become skilled in it, and the practitioner supports them in the process of applying cognitive change to specific irrational beliefs. But while the focus is on helping clients to use disputation for the specific irrational belief that pertains to their ongoing or presenting issue/s, in REBT we are also helping the client to fortify themselves against future (and inevitable) As. We are expressly encouraging clients to take learnings away from the specific work we are going into their general life. It is hoped and intended that by developing a rational way of seeing oneself and the world, that the client can approach all manner of events with an already instilled rational lens through which to view adversity. So in the moment, in the face of a real A, it is less that the client always consciously engages in disputation, and more that their wholesale approach to adversity is conducive to a rational interpretation – therefore enabling an implicit antecedent-focussed emotion regulation strategy that is less deliberative.

In sum, the rationale and purpose of disputation is twofold: a) systematic disputation is more likely to ensure that the client's irrational beliefs are comprehensively challenged and pilloried, and b) while undergoing disputation, the client is learning how to challenge their beliefs beyond the confines of the work you are doing together. Disputation is an important life-skill that stretches beyond the specifics of the issues that the client is currently experiencing. Therefore, it is important to teach the client the how, what, and why of disputation, in the interest of helping them develop their meta-cognitive abilities.

Scientists in cahoots

In disputation, the nature of the relationship between practitioner and client is important, and as was stressed earlier in the book, should be characterized in part by a "scientists in cahoots" approach to the client's issues. Beck and colleagues (e.g., Beck & Emery, 1985) refer to this therapeutic relationship as "collaborative empiricism", which is considered a critical element in the effectiveness of CBT per se (e.g., Kuyken et al., 2009). Clark (2014) indicates that collaborative empiricism involves the practitioner and client sharing their expertise in order to resolve the client's issues. The client is an expert in their lived experience, and the practitioner is an expert in the human change process, so they can work together in the cognitive change process to ensure the best solutions are arrived at for the client. In REBT, the practitioner encourages the client to be critical about their ideas and beliefs, and to question the veracity, logic, and usefulness of their internal states (i.e., inferences, beliefs, emotions), with an acute focus on irrational beliefs for specific REBT to be achieved.

Disputation should be imbued with this scientific approach to beliefs and belief change, such that clients can learn to recognize dis-confirming evidence for their irrational beliefs, to realize that their irrational beliefs do not help them attain their goals, and to generate and strengthen alternative rational beliefs that do help them. One method I have found important for the objectivism required for scientific analyses of beliefs, is to encourage the client to externalize the irrational beliefs so that the belief can be to some extent separated from the individual (i.e., "you are not your beliefs"). This can aid the scientific approach to the irrational belief in part because it is more palatable for the client to challenge *their beliefs* rather than *themselves*. It is *the belief* that is challenged and disputed, not *the individual* holding the belief. The belief can be physically written down in order to provide a tangible expression of the beliefs to which we can target our disputes. By helping the client to understand that they are not their beliefs, and that their beliefs are not precious, we can more rigorously dispute the beliefs and help the client to understand that their beliefs can be challenged just like anything else in this world.

The following content provides some guidance on the ways in which disputation can be conducted with clients. None of these methods are prescriptions and they do not need to be (and perhaps should not be) used in isolation.

Start at C

Think about any meaningful journey (an actual one, not a metaphorical one). You decide where you want to go (which is usually underpinned by a *why* too), and then you decide how you are going to get there. This logic can be applied to disputation, and we can ask the client, "How would you like to feel? How would you like to behave? What feelings and actions would serve your goals most effectively?"

We can use the information we have about the UNE to help here, "Currently, you say you are experiencing unhealthy anxiety concerning A. But how do you *want* to feel about A?". The client might say they want to feel "relaxed", and between you, you will need to figure out whether being relaxed is the most functional approach to A or not. This can be done by figuring out the *why*. But usually, healthy anxiety (rather than no anxiety at all) captures the gravity of the A while holding some functional, helpful tenets (e.g., preparation, focus). So, client and practitioner arrive at a position where there is a want and a will to move from a specific UNE (current location), to a specific HNE (desired destination).

Assuming the practitioner has introduced the client to the GABC aspects of the framework, we can ask the client what they think is the best option to getting from UNE to HNE. For example, we might say

> Let's say you want to go from this unhealthy anxiety you are experiencing, to experiencing healthy anxiety. Knowing what you now know about the GABCs of REBT, what do you think is the best way to get from the UNE to the HNE?

Obviously, what you are looking for here is an intimation that the client recognizes that their irrational belief could be changed, and if the client suggests that A needs to change, you can converse about the upsides and downsides of this approach. Ultimately, client and practitioner should arrive at the position that to get from UNE to HNE, a good solution might be irrational belief change (although, "change" is not quite accurate here, because we don't change the belief per se, but we do weaken it and offer up a new belief), and that there is a method we can apply to help this journey to take place. We can then explain disputation, detail the steps we can take, and then importantly, get the client's permission to go ahead with disputation. The client may have a range of irrational beliefs that have been identified, so just focus on one at a time, and get the client's direction and approval when deciding which to focus on and in what order (e.g., Dryden, 2019b).

Some final points before I go on – in specific REBT disputation is applied *only* to the irrational and rational beliefs, not to Gs, As or Cs. In terms of ordering, I have found it preferable to dispute the irrational belief/s, develop rational alternative belief/s, and then dispute the rational alternative beliefs (DiGiuseppe, 1991). This is known as consecutive (IB then RB) disputation (Dryden, 2019b).

Disputation arguments

> "*Anger will cease and become more controllable if it finds that it must appear before a judge every day*"
>
> -Seneca (2010)

If you have read even just some of the volumes of practical works concerning REBT, you will have undoubtedly come across the empirical (true or false?), logical (sensical or nonsensical?), and pragmatic (helpful or unhelpful?)

disputation arguments. Without doubt, they are the most commonly written about and recommended disputational arguments in the REBT canon, and thus, I will cover these first. These arguments are predicated on the notion that irrational beliefs are false (and could not be true), and/or nonsensical (inconsistent with reality), and/or unhelpful (self-destructive). Irrational beliefs boast no empirical evidence in support of their veracity, reflect illogical non-sequiturs, and hinder goal attainment. In contrast, rational beliefs are true, sensical, and helpful. Rational beliefs boast empirical evidence in support of their veracity (or at least *could* be true), reflect logical sequiturs, and aid goal attainment. So, the empirical, logical, and pragmatic disputation arguments are indelibly tied to the defining features of irrational and rational beliefs. Practically, the practitioner is asking the client to a) posit some evidence attesting to the truth or falsity of the belief (empirical), b) consider whether the target belief (both irrational and rational) is logical or not, c) and consider the functionality or helpfulness of the target belief (Dryden & Branch, 2008; Neenan & Dryden, 1999b). That is, the practitioner *asks*, not tells. Scientists *in cahoots* (alliance or partnership). Disputation largely applies logical-empirical methods of science (Dryden & Branch, 2008) through the use of questions (DiGiuseppe et al., 2014). Below, I offer some of the questions that work well for me, and I focus on demands ("I want it, therefore I must have it"), since comprehensive guidelines exist elsewhere that cover all kinds of belief types (e.g., DiGiuseppe et al., 2014; Dryden, 2019b; Dryden & Branch, 2008; Ellis, 1994; Neenan & Dryden, 1999b).

Empirical

- Where is the evidence that you MUST get what you want?
- Where is it written that you MUST get what you want?
- Can you provide some data or evidence to support your demand?
- Is there a rule somewhere that dictates that you MUST get what you want?
- What universal law exists that says you MUST get what you want?
- Have there been times when you didn't get what you wanted? So how can your demand to get what you want be true?
- What things MUST you have or do in life? (client answers usually: air, water, food, sleep). Does being approved of by your friend fit into the same category as these musts and have to's?
- Has your demand ensured that you get what you always get what you want? Is there evidence that you do not get what you want, even when you demand it?
- Is it possible that, despite your demand, you might not get what you want?
- Is it consistent with reality, that because you want something, then you MUST have it? Is that how the world works?
- What data can you use to support your demand?
- If your MUST is true, then whenever you use it, you would get what you want. Is this always the case?

Logical

- You said that you want X, *and therefore*, you MUST have it. Is that good logic?
- So, when you want something, you get to demand it? Is this how the world really works?
- Does it follow that just because you want something, then you HAVE TO have it?
- How do you get from *wanting* X, to *demanding* X?
- If you heard someone else making a similar argument that because they wanted something, that it must be, would you be convinced?
- Where is the logic in saying that because you want something, then you MUST have it?
- Can you explain to me how you get from wanting X, to demanding X?
- Why do you *have to* have it, just because you *want* it?
- I see why you might WANT it, but does that necessarily mean that you MUST have it?
- You might want it more than anything else in the world, but does that mean you get to demand it?
- If you faced an opponent, and they demanded the same as you, do you both get to win?
- Are you some of omnipotent Monarch? In your life, do you just demand things and then automatically get them?

Pragmatic

- Where has your belief that you "MUST have it" got you?
- Has demanding that you MUST have it helped you to achieve your goals?
- Is demanding that you MUST have it helping you or hindering you?
- How has *demanding* you get what you want, actually helped you to get what you want?
- How is your demand that you MUST get it working for you?
- If your demand that you MUST have it was helping you, do you think you would have asked for my help?
- "Whatever I want, I must get". Where will that command get you?
- Is it worth it for you to hold on to the belief that "I must get what I want"?
- When you demand that you get what you want, how do you feel?. . . And is that feeling helpful to you?
- What happens to you when you demand that you MUST have what you want?
- If you were to list all the ways this demand has helped you versus hindered you, which list would be longest?
- If you didn't demand that you MUST get what you want, would that really stop you from getting what you want?

The pragmatic dispute is particularly powerful, in part because it speaks to the utilitarian in people, and uselessness is a real blow for most ideas. The list above is not prescriptive or exhaustive, but gives an idea of the way in which practitioners can approach disputation arguments.

As with anything in life, disputation can be done badly. It is important not to be pedantic or condescending when using disputation arguments. Approaching disputation in a condescending and arrogant ("I know better than you") is likely to damage the working alliance, and damage the client's confidence in debating and sharing with you. Given the breadth of available arguments, the practitioner selects the appropriate questions/statements based on their knowledge of the client and their issues (including their Gs, As, Bs, and Cs), their rapport with the client, and on their confidence in applying the arguments. Don't dig yourself a hole with your disputation, because you will confuse yourself, and your client! Also, timing is very important in disputation, and due to the meta-cognitive nature of what we are asking the client to do, it is advisable to allow the client time to process the questions you pose and consider their response. This might mean there are some silent pauses in the conversation, which the practitioner should embrace. It is also important that the practitioner encourages the client to answer the *actual* question, rather than answering the question they *want* to answer. Don't let them wriggle out of these disputations, which they may do because they are uncomfortable or defensive of their long-held belief. The practitioner need not rush, and it is better to execute disputation rigorously and thoroughly rather than see it as tick box exercise. What the client learns here, in terms of the ability to dispute, they can apply to the rest of their lives.

Figure 9.1 Client belief disputation

Socratic comparison

In my experience, the disputation arguments are very effective in helping the client to work against their irrational beliefs. However, usually I will not rely solely on these arguments to dispute irrational beliefs. Socratic comparison starts to help the client to understand the differences in truth, logic, and function between rational and irrational beliefs by providing examples for them to grapple with, or by using their own rational and irrational beliefs, to compare and contrast. One of the reasons that these comparison tasks work well is because they create some cognitive dissonance (e.g., Festinger, 1957, 1962) in the client, whereby the contradictory nature of the rational versus irrational beliefs leads to psychological discomfort. The client is motived to reduce this dissonance, and therefore the process of instantiating rational beliefs is aided through the desire for internal consistency.

One approach to Socratic comparison is to use paired comparisons. In this approach the practitioner questions paired components of the client's irrational belief and rational belief, at the same time (Neenan & Dryden, 1999b). This activity has clients consider their irrational beliefs in comparison to the rational alternative. As you can see in Figure 9.2, the client's irrational belief is in the middle column, and the identified rational belief is in the right column next to it. The practitioner then asks the client:

- Which belief is true and which is false?
- Which belief is sensible/logical and which doesn't make sense or is illogical?
- Which belief is helpful and which is unhelpful?
- Which of the two beliefs do you want to strengthen and act on?

The client then places a tick in the box that reflects their answer. As with previous methods, engage the client in discussion as to their decision making, and ensure that they are clear in their reasons for their answers. No need to rush. Each irrational belief identified with the client (e.g., demands, awfulizing) should be submitted to this comparison separately, but variations of the task are put forth by Neenan and Dryden (1999b). This activity helps the work to move towards strengthening the rational belief, and importantly, provides some rationale for doing so.

Another type of comparison task I like to use is what I call the "multiple yous" task. In this activity you have the client imagine that there are multiple versions of themself ('multiple yous') in the future; you A and you B. Here is the twist though – you A holds irrational beliefs about the self, others, the world, whereas you B holds rational beliefs about the self, others, the world. Then I ask the client to run a simulation in their head for "you A" and "you B" sequentially. How does life pan out for you A if irrational beliefs are maintained and left to prosper? In contrast, how does life pan out for you B if rational beliefs are developed, strengthened, and maintained? This is a very abstract task, but does clearly highlight to the client that they are at a crossroad at this point in time and get to decide which of these "yous" they want to embody. The driving motivation for using Socratic comparison is to pit irrational beliefs against rational beliefs to increase cognitive dissonance and aid disputation.

	Rational "I want to succeed, but I do not have to"	Irrational "I want to succeed, and therefore I have to"
Which belief is true and which is false?		
Which belief is sensible/logical and which doesn't make sense or is illogical?		
Which belief is helpful and which is unhelpful?		
Which of the two beliefs do you want to strengthen and act on?		

Figure 9.2 Paired components rating disputation task

Disputation styles

In much of the REBT literature, the style of disputation is boiled down to two main approaches: Socratic versus didactic. But it is common to use a range or combination of styles that suit the client, and the two styles can be used in conjunction.

Socratic. The practitioner asks the client focused, open, and meaningful questions, many of which are illustrated earlier in this section, concerning the empirical, logical and pragmatic status of their irrational and rational beliefs. An excellent discussion can be found in DiGiuseppe et al. (2014, pp. 171–173). This style is preferable to engender client self-discovery and practitioner-client collaboration. One of the ways in which we can execute this style is to humbly act as though the client can actually teach us something we don't know. This is of course a truism, because we really know almost nothing about the client and therefore we should approach them with an inquisitive frame of mind thus allowing and encouraging them to explain to us what they believe and the foundations for these beliefs. Within the context of disputation, this means we can act as if we do not understand the empirical, logical, and pragmatic foundations of the beliefs they hold. With an irrational belief like "I want, therefore I must, be respected by my peers" we might question the logic of the belief by saying to the client "I don't quite understand here. Please explain to me how you get a must from a want" or "help me to figure this out. How are you going from 'want' to 'must'?"

Didactic. The practitioner tells the client, using short explanations and examples, why their irrational beliefs are irrational, and their rational beliefs are rational (e.g., Neenan & Dryden, 1999b). This is really a form of psychoeducation (e.g., Sarracino et al., 2017), a method often used when time is of the essence or the work is conducted in a group format (e.g., Turner & Davis, 2019). This style is also useful with clients who cannot engage with Socratic disputing (Dryden, 2019b). Dryden (2009a, 2009b) suggest that this style is used in short chunks, using visual aids, in the client's language, with the practitioner checking for client understanding as they go. This second approach is for sure less preferable and perhaps less advantageous for the work, and I would always prize self-revelation and realization over a didactic style. But, as REBT practitioners we are pragmatists, and would not labour a Socratic approach if there are indications that it is not effective with the client.

Summary

In this section I have covered ways in which the practitioner can dispute (D) clients' irrational and rational beliefs (B), in order to help them learn the skills of questioning and challenging their beliefs, and to help the client address their current UNEs. I have touched upon how disputation can be applied, and the styles that characterize disputation. Next, I move onto discussing the development and strengthening of effective new rational beliefs (E), which is the next logical step after successful disputation.

10 Effective new beliefs (E)

One of the best examples of the adoption of effective beliefs I can think of is Rory McIlroy (who has won six gold majors to date) laying out his performance mindset, taken from interviews given by Rory McIlroy in April of 2019 (Cannizzaro, 2019; Jackson, 2019; Jones, 2019). In support of rational preference beliefs, Rory states

> I would have said a couple of years ago, "I need to win a Masters. I need a green jacket". But now it's, "I want to. I want to win it. And I'd love to win it", but if I don't then I'm okay with that. And I think that is the difference.

In support of anti-awfulizing, he states "I would dearly love to win this tournament again one day, if it doesn't happen this week that's totally fine, I'll come back next year". In support of unconditional self-acceptance, he asserts that "I am not my score. I am not my results. Its perspective, its perception" and "I don't define myself by who I am as a golfer anymore. I'm very comfortable with who I am as a person and very comfortable with who I am as a golfer". These extracts from interviews with Rory McIlroy are snapshots of the rational approach he is taking to golf, and he seems to be doing ok (!) But McIlroy did not always approach golf in this way, he had to work hard to develop this approach. So how do we as practitioners help our clients to develop this rational approach to life? This is the focus of E, and the focus of this chapter.

Developing rational beliefs

Some of the work necessary for E has already been started in D. Depending on the methods that the practitioner uses in D, rational alternative beliefs may have been posited, and perhaps even disputed. Remember, in REBT we are not *changing* the irrational beliefs per se; rather, we are weakening the conviction in irrational beliefs, and strengthening the conviction in rational beliefs. Disputation is applied to both irrational and rational beliefs, using in essence the same arguments. There are variations in how much E is done alongside D, but I consider E to be explicitly about clearly defining new rational beliefs, and helping the client to strengthen their conviction in, and application of, rational beliefs. When helping the client to

DOI: 10.4324/9781003508472-11

develop their effective new rational beliefs at E, there are some considerations we must take.

First, will new rational beliefs be decided on collaboratively, or will the practitioner take a more didactic approach? The former is preferred in order to ensure ownership of the new beliefs and to ensure the client's choice of precise words is considered. Second, how comprehensive and articulated will the new beliefs be? While it is more appealing to instantiate the belief that "I can tolerate it" because it is snappy and short, it does not capture the full rational belief ("It is tough, but I can tolerate it, and it is worth it to do so"). The latter is preferred, even though it is more long-winded. Accuracy is vital here, because it is important that the belief to which the client will commit is aligned with the core tenets of rationality laid out in REBT. But over time, the client can shorten this belief so long as the essence is still captured and client understands the deep rationality that underpins their shorter and catchier self-talk. For example, the client can use symbolic language that more efficiently captures their rational beliefs. Third, given the often long and winding conversations that can take place in REBT (although we try not to let this happen), despite its structured and focussed nature, it could be advantageous to go back through what has been covered so far. So, if required, recap the G-D journey you have been on in your work together. This can ensure the client, and the practitioner, is clear on why the E stage is to be executed at this point. Lastly, make time for E and ensure that the client is ready for it. I try to ensure that E is started in a new session, rather than at the end of a session. This allows the client to reflect meaningfully on how we have arrived at this point, and assuming that D has just taken place, it is worth allowing D to sink in before beginning E.

Extending the latter point, readiness for E is also about being prepared for a long-term commitment to rationality. This requires ongoing effort from the client, and they can anticipate and plan for some backsliding into their old ways of thinking even as they strengthen their conviction and commitment to the effective new belief over time. Indeed, clients might be able to quickly understand the effective new beliefs, and also experience some of the short-term benefits of holding them, but committing to internalizing these beliefs and holding them long-term is a more difficult task. Ideally, the effective new beliefs should be automatized, such that they inform the client's natural and habitual healthy response to adversity. This automatization requires rehearsal, repetition, and reinforcement, just like the automatization of a physical skill. Ellis (1976) recognized that change in irrational beliefs can be short-lived unless one is dedicated to the ongoing disputation of such ideas, and states that "When modifications and/or eliminations of certain irrationalities do occur, changes in the frequency, intensity, and duration of these irrationalities are often short-lived, thus resulting in regression, relapse, and/or newly acquired and invented ones" (in Ruth, 1992, p. 6).

It is not a good idea to try to obliterate irrational beliefs, and then leave a void, because irrational beliefs can creep back in and fill the void. We need to help the client to develop convincing arguments for their rational beliefs that render the irrational beliefs surplus to requirements and fill the gap that disputation leaves.

Also, because people often have rational beliefs alongside irrational beliefs (Ellis, 2002a), it is advantageous to ensure that when rational beliefs are developed, they negate the irrational belief as well as state clearly the rational elements (e.g., I want to, *but I do not have to*") (DiGiuseppe et al., 1988). The best way to construct a rational belief is to negate the irrational belief. In this way, we integrate the irrational within the rational such that we do not deny or ignore the irrational aspects, but recognize and explicitly counter them. We say "it is bad, *but not terrible*" or "I want, *but I do not have to*", for example.

It is important to note that rationality and irrationality can be viewed as two separate dials (Figures 10.1 and 10.2) on a sound system, like bass and treble. Bass and treble are separate, but interact, and can be adjusted independently, just like irrational and rational beliefs. Irrational and rational beliefs are not at opposite ends of the same continuum (Bernard, 2009), they are separate, but interacting. It is not that we are *changing* the irrational *to* rational. We are not *swapping* the bass *for the* treble. We are dialling down the bass (i.e., irrational beliefs), and dialling up the treble (i.e., rational beliefs). The bass will always be there – it is a ubiquitous aspect of human nature – but so will the treble. We can help clients to become skilled mixers by teaching them skills that will help them to dial down the bass and dial up the treble when required.

Emotional insight

In REBT, we are striving for *emotional* insight, not just *intellectual* insight. On completion of D the client may have developed some *intellectual* insight into the nature of rational and irrational beliefs, the key differences between them (as it pertains to the client's particularly issues), and the way disputation

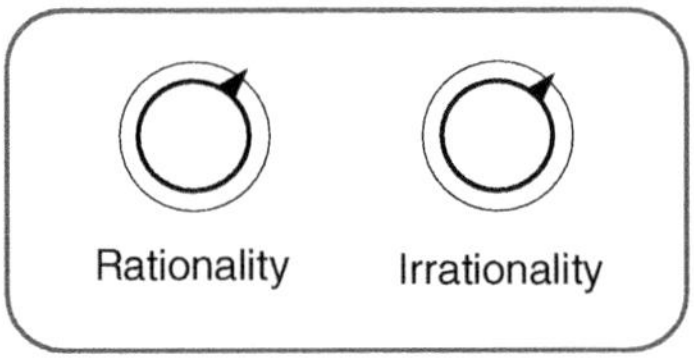

Figure 10.1 Rational/irrational frequency dials

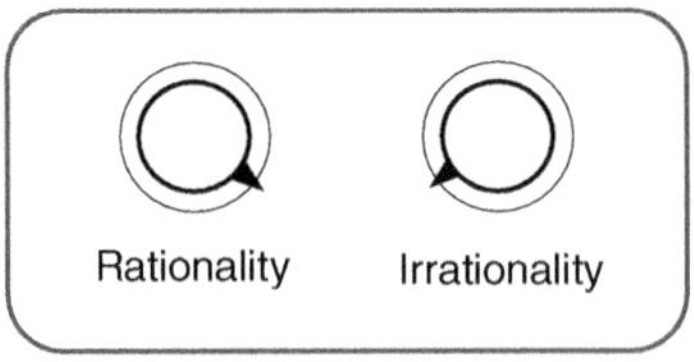

Figure 10.2 High rationality and low irrationality on the rational/irrational frequency dials

can be used per se (Dryden, 2018). The client acknowledges that their beliefs are underpinning their unhealthy negative emotions (UNE). But *intellectual* insight is usually not enough alone to impact the client's emotions and behaviours in a meaningful way, and the client has not yet made a consistent effort to change (Ellis, 1963). Indeed, the client may still truly believe the irrational beliefs, and while they can see why the rational beliefs are indeed more constructive, they will only lightly believe these rational beliefs. Thus, we need to help the client to work towards *emotional* insight to facilitate meaningful change, which involves the client committing to the rational beliefs and committing to the work that is required for meaningful change (Ellis, 1963). In other words, D and E should be life skills that the client can commit to over the life course, rather than remedial short-term techniques that are forgotten about as soon as the REBT work ceases with the client. In other words, if you want to develop rational beliefs, then you must work to believe rationally, and work against believing irrationally (Bernard, 2009).

Rather than seeing E as just the development of new rational beliefs, I also see it as the strengthening and committing to this new rationality. So next, I move on to discussing some of the more prominent and common methods through which rational beliefs are promoted and reinforced at E. As with disputation (D), a combination of methods should be used to enhance the effectiveness of our E work.

Promoting and reinforcing rational beliefs

Rational cue cards

It is important that the new rational beliefs are constructed to be technically accurate to REBT, but also written in the client's language as much as possible (DiGiuseppe et al., 2014). By that, I mean that the rational beliefs should reflect preferences, anti-awfulizing, FT, and or unconditional acceptance, but should be written in words that the client understands and connects with. When this is the case, producing cue cards with the rational beliefs printed or written on them is a useful strategy for helping the client to internalize the rational beliefs. Ten cue cards can be placed in ten different areas that the client will frequently visit. For example, the client can place one in their kit bag, wallet, purse, bedside draw, glove compartment in car, etc. The idea here is to have the client place the cue cards in places where they will happen upon them, therefore seeing and reading (even unconsciously) the rational beliefs frequently and unavoidably. This is not a long-term strategy, but serves as a short-term way of helping the client to remember and rehearse the rational beliefs until they believe that it has been internalized. The same type of activity can be achieved using a Smartphone by setting up a calendar alarm each day with the rational belief as the title of the appointment. Clients can also use the Smarter Thinking App (Turner & Wood, 2019a) to access their chosen rational beliefs to aid reflection and internalization.

Rational Credo

A credo is "a set of beliefs, which expresses a particular opinion and influences the way you live" (Dryden, 2007, p. 219). Specifically, the Rational Resilience Credo was developed by Dryden (2007) as a set of rational beliefs born from REBT theory, promoting an ideal resilient response to adversity. In 2016, I adapted the credo to suit the audience with whom I apply the credo, i.e., athletes. I developed the Athlete Rational Resilience Credo (ARRC; Turner, 2016a), based on Dryden's (2007) credo, but adapted it to a performance audience. The ARRC has been used in research to support the application of REBT (Chrysidis et al., 2020; Deen et al., 2017; Elvins et al., 2025). In Figure 10.3, I present a further adapted "Rational Credo" (based on Turner, 2020b) that is briefer than the one presented by Turner (2016a) and not specific to sport.

As a human being I have many desires or "wants". Some of these desires are very strong as I am driven to be the best person I can possibly be. However, I recognize that no matter how strong my desires are this does not mean that I "have to" or "must" have my desires met. I may want to be successful, be accepted, be treated well, and keep developing my skills, but I know that these desires do not "have to" be met. I accept that from time to time my desires will not be met. It's OK that I feel upset and disappointed when my desires are not met, as this shows that I care about my life and my development. My upset feelings are normal, and they can motivate me to work hard towards my desires, knowing full well that demanding that these desires are met is rigid, nonsensical, and fruitless. Not having my wants met provides me with opportunities to grow as a person, fully accepting that unfavourable events are valuable even though they may lead to unpleasant feelings.

I recognize that when my desires are not met, I fail, face setbacks, this is inconvenient and unfortunate but not terrible or the end of the world. No matter how bad it is to not have my desires met, I know that worse things could and have happened to me, none of which are truly awful. It is difficult to face adversity to my important goals, but I know that this adversity is never truly awful. Further, if I am not given opportunities, this certainly is not the end of the world. Even though I might feel upset and my goal attainment may be hindered, I can distinguish inconvenience from catastrophe. I accept that bad things will happen, and that's OK as this provides me with valuable opportunities to grow as a person.

Not having my desires met is very tough and difficult to tolerate. But I know I can tolerate this, because not getting what I want will not kill me or cause so much pain that I disintegrate. Even if my strongest desires are not met, it is not unbearable. To not meet my goals is very hard but I know that I can certainly stand this. Although I may feel frustrated and upset and my goal attainment may be hindered, I know that I have the capacity to tolerate failure, setbacks, and being let down. Importantly, I accept that facing tough situations that do not meet my desires is OK as this provides me with valuable opportunities to grow and develop as a person. Ultimately, being able to tolerate adversity is worthwhile because of the strength it gives me to face future adversity. However, just because I can tolerate adversity, it does not mean that I will tolerate it. I can pick my battles, and I if I know something is wrong, I can protest and remonstrate.

If I fail to reach a goal, or if I face an obstacle, I recognize that this is bad, but it says nothing about me as a person. I know that failing does not make me a failure, that stumbling on the way to a goal does not make me useless, and does not mean I am worthless. Similarly, succeeding does not mean I am a success, a smooth path to my goal does not mean I am perfect, and does not make me a worthy person. I am able to distinguish between my own behaviour, and me as a total human being. I am not what I do. I am worthwhile because I am human, not because I am good at certain things in my life. When I fall short, it just shows that I am a fallible human being just like all other humans. Sometimes I succeed, sometimes I fail, and that's fine. It's OK to feel upset when I fail, face setbacks, or am let down. These feelings can motivate me to work on aspects of myself that are hindering me. No matter how bad things are, I realize that life is a mixture of good and bad events, and that the bad events test me and provide valuable opportunities to develop as a person.

Figure 10.3 The rational credo

The ARRC comprises one paragraph for each of the core rational beliefs; paragraph one covers preferences, and paragraphs two, three, and four cover anti-awfulizing, FT, and unconditional acceptance, respectively. The ARRC assertively promotes the four core rational beliefs, which has three main advantages. The ARRC gives a clear indication of what clients can aim for in terms of achieving a rational philosophy of life, focusses on the utility of beliefs, rather than changes in G or A, which promotes B-C connections and dissuades A-C connections, and it is written in the first person – rather than speaking to the client, as the client reads it, they speak to *themselves*.

I suggest three main methods of using the ARRC with clients. First, clients can work to internalize the full credo by reading and rehearsing each day – they could even record the credo on their Smartphone to listen to. Practice makes permanent. Second, the client can select chunks of text that are most germane to their issues and or goals for use as self-talk – they could create some cue cards with shorter sections on them. Third, clients can produce their own ARRC using the generic ARRC as a template. This creates some ownership over the ARRC, can be written using the client's idiosyncratic language, and encourages critical engagement in REBT – the client has to properly understand and be able to articulate REBT in order to create their credo.

Rational self-talk

Of course, the strategies covered thus far in the chapter all make use of self-talk in one way or another. Rational self-talk, or rational self-statements, have been used in past research to formulate rational conditions in which the participants are provided with a set of rational statements to rehearse and use on approach to a task. Examples of rational and irrational self-talk can be seen in Figure 10.4, which are taken from a study with golfers. In the study, after controlling for the participants playing ability (i.e., baseline scores), data showed that the golfers who adopted rational self-statements recorded higher putting accuracy compared to when engaging with irrational alternatives.

Rational self-talk or self-statements can be used on approach to a task in order to maximize task execution. Dryden (2019a) suggests, and I agree, that encouraging the client to actually face their As while rehearsing their rational beliefs is a very powerful technique. When encouraging the client to do this, it is important they refrain from avoiding the A or removing themselves from A before they have successful regulated their emotion by using the rational belief. This mixture of behavioural intent to face A and not avoid it, and the cognitive strategy of using the rational beliefs, creates a powerful inoculation effect against the threat of A. For example, perhaps a driving student is unhealthily anxious about making errors in the car (A), so has been avoiding driving lessons (C) and ignoring their instructors text messages. The student has an irrational belief that "I must not make errors in the car, and if I do make mistakes it shows how useless I am". I would encourage the student to rehearse the belief that "I would prefer not to make errors in the car, but if I do make mistakes, it is not ideal, but it doesn't mean that I am useless, it just shows I am fallible like everyone else!" while forthrightly going on their lessons and engaging with their instructor.

A modification of this technique would be to have the client enter into the commitment of taking extra lessons and going out driving with a responsible adult, without the rehearsal of the rational belief. Just like the story about Albert Ellis in New York Botanical Gardens that opened this book, by acting differently, you can think differently. The exposure to A and encouragement to "stay in there" (Dryden, 2019b) is sometimes known as "flooding" (e.g., Ellis, 1980; Turner et al., 2020b), and can help the client to realize that the situation is not as bad as they thought it was, and that if they do make mistakes, nobody really notices or cares. Even if people do notice and care, the client will notice that they are still capable of driving successfully in many aspects, and are thus not "useless". These experiences will help the client to develop and reinforce the rational belief because they have gathered empirical evidence to disprove the irrational belief, and prove the rational belief. So, this technique can help the client to re-appraise A (i.e., inferential A change), and or develop rational beliefs; either way, they are able to face the

Rational self-talk	Irrational self-talk
I want to sink this putt but that doesn't mean I must	I want to sink this putt and therefore I must
If I don't succeed in this task, it will be bad but not awful	If I don't succeed in this task it would be awful
If I don't succeed in this task, I will not like it, but I will be able to stand it	I would not be able to stand failing in this task
If I fail to sink this putt then I will have failed, but that would not make me a failure	If I miss this putt, it would make me a failure

Figure 10.4 Rational and irrational self-talk

situation forthrightly. The client will realize that the more they voluntarily face A, the more than will be able to face many other As.

A final point to make with regards to self-talk, is to not underestimate the utility of evocation and intonation (DiGiuseppe et al., 2014). When the client uses the rational beliefs, and when you help them to reinforce the rational beliefs, it is often useful to annunciate the key words like "must" versus "want", for example. Is it often the case that clients think that their rational beliefs should reflect calm and balance, which can be the case, but is not always true. For example, on facing an important event, it is fine to express the passion in wanting to perform well by evocatively expressing that "I REALLY WANT to perform well, but I do not HAVE TO". The words in capital letters can be higher or lower in pitch, louder, slowed down, and or enunciated. This can work out loud, or in the client's head. Don't be afraid to use expletives too (!) if the client is game.

Imagery

The client rehearses the new rational beliefs while they imagine themselves facing the adversity (Dryden, 2019b). The client does this until they can experience the healthy negative emotions (HNE). The practitioner may need to help the client develop their imagery skills first, but for some emotions, such as anxiety, the client is often quite apt at foreseeing their demise in light of A. Do not expect the client to be able to do this perfectly at first, and you can guide them in and out of imagery and build up to being able to experience HNE via the rational belief. Importantly, this method is helping the client to develop their self-efficacy in using their rational beliefs in the face of the adversity, and get used to feeling negative but healthy emotions as a result. In addition, Rational Emotive Imagery (REI; Maultsby, 1971) is an oft-used technique in REBT (Ellis & Harper, 1975; Hickey & Doyle, 2018; Hymen & Warren, 1978), which is a form of mental practice or rehearsal of thinking, feeling and behaving exactly the way you want (Maultsby, 1984). REI involves the client imagining the A and the UNE that it is associated with, and then changing the UNE to the HNE. The client then reports to the practitioner how they were able to go from UNE to HNE – if it was achieved by changing A, the client does this exercise again. The exercise continues until the client can change UNE to HNE by only changing their beliefs from irrational to rational. Once this is achieved, the client can practice this technique independently, now able to rehearse cognitive change in the service of the HNE. It is recommended that clients undertake REI for ten minutes, four or more times per day, but also more informally when they have time and opportunity (Wirga et al., 2020). In brief, the client is encouraged to alter their irrational beliefs to rational beliefs in order to alter their emotion, specifically, from UNE to HHE

One approach to REI uses the convergence of REBT and Lazarus' (1999) cognitive appraisal theory (covered earlier in this book) (Chadha et al., 2019). For example, knowing anger stems from a core relational theme of "misdemeanour against me and mine" (other blame), and appraisal components high goal relevance, and high goal incongruence, other/world-accountability, and or self-accountability, it is possible to have the client imagine the A to include these elements. Then, they can practice applying their rational belief in these types of situations in the service of healthy anger (HNE) as opposed to unhealthy anger (UNE). A good knowledge of theory can reveal useful applied techniques. While literature offers some very useful modes of imagery, for a specific REBT solution the focus should remain on belief change, rather than G and A change or direct C change.

If-then plans

Implementation intentions were posited by Dr Peter M. Gollwitzer, Professor of Psychology at New York University, and are more commonly known as "if-then plans", which are specific plans that identify both an appropriate goal-directed response and a suitable situation in which to initiate that response ("If situation *Y* arises, then I will perform goal directed behavior *Z*!"; Webb & Sheeran, 2007). This technique is quite simple and can be used to help clients to utilize the GAB-CDE framework out in the real world (e.g., Bishop, 2000), but from my experience is most useful for rehearsing the new rational beliefs (E). In implementation intentions, the "if" part could reflect the A (adversity, barrier, obstacle) that could thwart a goal (G), or it could reflect the goal (G) itself. The "then" part reflects the functional response to the A or G. In our case when using REBT, the "then" part is where we inject the client's newly developed rational beliefs.

For example, on approaching a competitive situation in which performing well is your aim (G), you could say "IF I feel unhealthily anxious before the competition, THEN I will remind myself that although I really want to perform well, that doesn't mean that I have to". Or, in situations where you are faced with social conflict (A), you could say "IF I am treated with disrespect, THEN I will reaffirm to myself that being treated with disrespect is tough, but I can tolerate it and it is worth it to do so." The client can make these if-then plans broader too, to reflect their fundamental goals (FGs). For example, "IF I want to fulfil my potential as a human being, THEN I will remind myself each day that although life is difficult and challenging, I can bear it and it is worth it to do so". Or,

> IF I want to maintain my healthy emotional disposition, THEN each day I will tell myself that I am a fallible human being that sometimes succeeds, and sometimes fails, and that my self-worth is not contingent on this success and failure.

Implementation intentions are more useful for clients than just assuming or expecting that they will apply their rational beliefs in relevant situations. If-then plans give them a strategy and well, a plan (!), with which to go forthrightly into the real world. It is then less likely that they will be caught off guard in the face of an A, and slip back into their old irrationalities. The benefit of integrating REBT principles into the implementation intentions is that the THEN component is controllable by the client. It can even be used to apply to REBT itself, for example, "IF I find myself demanding the things that I want, THEN I will challenge my thinking with truth, logic, and pragmatics". There are of course many potential IF's and many possible THEN's, so you can help the client to formulate and test these if-then plans in session, and encourage them to apply them as homework assignments. As the client practices this planning more frequently, they will develop more confidence in applying their new rational beliefs across a range of situations. They feel prepared for the As that await them, and the As they themselves bring forth.

Debate and role play

One very useful way to help the client to reinforce their rational beliefs, is to have the client defend them. For example, you can engage the client in a debate concerning the rational beliefs in which you argue *against* the rational belief, and they argue *for* the rational belief. You can also reverse these roles so that the client is *against* the rational belief, and the practitioner is *for* the rational beliefs (DiGiuseppe et al., 2014). Indeed, the client can make use of an intrapersonal dialogue between two parts of the self, rational versus irrational, to promote commitment to the rational (Dryden, 2018). One way to do this is to have the client argue both for and against using a two-chair technique (Dryden, 2019b). When the client sits in one chair they argue *against* the rational belief, and when they sit in the other chair, they argue *for* the rational belief. The practitioner moderates the "debate" and encourages both sides to use the principles of evidence, logic, and pragmatics. Whichever format is selected, the practitioner should take sufficient time to set this up properly, and to help the client reflect on the meaning of this work after it has been completed. What we are doing here is encouraging the independent utilization of disputation, and at the same time bolstering the client's commitment to the rational beliefs.

How do we know E is working?

The client may be able to comprehend that their irrational beliefs are hindering them, and that rational beliefs would better serve them. They may be able to very articulately grasp the differences between irrational and rational beliefs, and understand disputation. But, as many writers have noted, comprehension alone may not be sufficient to engender emotional and or behavioural change (e.g., Kinney, 2000). As mentioned earlier in this chapter, one of the hallmarks that REBT has worked, is that the client demonstrates *emotional* insight on top of their *intellectual* insight. This emotional insight can be demonstrated in many ways by the client, chief of which are a) the assumption of responsibility for thoughts, feelings, and actions, b) the clear and strong recognition that they can do something about their irrational beliefs and the long-term commitment to doing something about their irrational beliefs, c) the *independent* disputation of irrational beliefs and the acting against the irrational beliefs, and d) the spontaneous formulation of rational beliefs in the face of adversity. As Ellis (1963) puts it, "Where the client with intellectual-insight . . . thinks it would be desirable if he believed the right things, he does not actually believe them. The person with emotional insight truly believes, is committed, and therefore acts" (p. 126).

Intellectual insight is really best demonstrated at the level of behaviour. Is the client forthrightly taking on the A that typically gives rise to their Bs and UNEs? Is the client actively engaging socially? Is the client taking on new challenges? Is the client employing healthy coping strategies to deal with life's many challenges? In brief, is the client acting against the irrational belief? Given that we have a concept of what behavioural tenets help define HNEs, the practitioner can assess the expression of these behaviours, or action tendencies, to help infer whether emotional insight is being achieved.

To help the client achieve emotional insight, practitioners should not over rely on cognitive methods in their work (DiGiuseppe et al., 2014; Kinney, 2000). The use of emotive, imaginal, and behavioural methods is important here (e.g., Robb et al., 1999), and these activities can be done both in and out of sessions. For example, REI can be practitioner led, but the client can also apply this technique independently, so long as they have learned it properly in-session. Flooding, or "stay in there" techniques can be applied by the client out in the real world, or by using imagery, and can powerfully demonstrate that a feared stimulus is not "awful" and the client can in fact "tolerate" the adversity (DiGiuseppe et al., 2014).

Caring less

Some clients worry about rationality. Some believe that by being more rational, it means that you will become an unemotional, unmotivated, dispassionate, robot. There is this sense that irrationality and the emotional heat that it generates is somehow tied to how much a person cares about something, and thus, the removal of this irrationality will in some way damage their chances of getting that thing. How can they succeed in life if they do not care? Indeed, there is a misconception that wanting instead of demanding, not viewing failure as the end of the world, tolerating life's vicissitudes, and not defining yourself by your pursuits, is disadvantageous in part because of reductions in motivation (Atkinson, 2014).

This is obviously a very simplistic, and frankly worrying, view of REBT, emotion, and motivation. None of these concerns are borne out by the data, and in my applied work I have never had a client suffer from emotional or motivational deficits through my work with them. It is not the case that encouraging rational beliefs leads to lack of motivation, and we are not teaching clients to care less. We are not teaching them to be passive. We are not minimizing their desires for success, goal attainment, fulfilment of potential. We are merely enabling a balanced and healthy approach to those goals, shifting a desperate and panicked "must" to a more measured but equally passionate *want*. We can help them to care appropriately about those goals, and ensure that they do not sacrifice their well-being on the altar of vocational success.

Summary

In this chapter we have taken a look at the effective new beliefs (E) element of the GABCDE framework. If you and the client are successful in this element, then the client will likely be able to move into the future with the skills to pursue Gs and face As with rationality. Because of this, the client has markedly enhanced their proclivity to experience HNEs in pursuit of their goals, and as a result, has also enhanced the likelihood of attaining those goals. The client can apply the skills of disputation and rational belief strengthening to fortify themselves against the vicissitudes of life. The work for the client is not over, of course. Only continued commitment to rationality and constant work against irrationality will secure long-term fulfilment and psychological health.

11 Finishing the work, and closing remarks

At some stage, your work with the client must come to an end. Ideally, this work ends after the main tasks of REBT have been executed, but of course, work with clients can end prematurely for all sorts of reasons. I won't cover the multitude of different endings with clients, as this would take up an entire book. In contrast, if you are imbedded within a team as I often am, work between you and the client will only really finish when they or you leave the organization for which you are providing psychology support. This often means that you will complete the more intensive work with the client, but you are on hand to continue your support in a more causal manner as you continue your work at the organization. It is important to draw a line under the specific work you have been doing with an individual client, while also communicating that you are there to support them if they face further issues, or would just like a conversation with you. Of course, ending the work can be a joint decision (although obviously the client can stop whenever they want), and we are to avoid indelicately and abruptly drawing the work to a close. Just like many aspects of REBT, we are led by the client but offer guidance, and ending the work is no different. If you as a practitioner believe there is enough evidence that the client is ready to finish the work, and the client believes that they are ready to finish the work, then a perfect alignment has been reached.

Contextual and individual specifics notwithstanding, in this chapter I will briefly outline how the work should ideally end. In REBT, we are always looking towards the end (DiGiuseppe et al., 2014), because one of our main goals is to help clients to learn the skills of REBT so that they can use them independently into the future. It is never our aim to become a crutch for our clients, and while this might be a bad business model (!), it is an ethical stance as much as it is a part of the REBT philosophy of emotional responsibility. As we near the end of our work with a client, and indeed near the end of this book, here is a reminder of the main tasks of specific REBT:

1. Develop and strengthen the working alliance.
2. Establish the aims of the work, agree on a target problem, and a way forward.
3. Assess C – establish the existence of UNEs and HNEs concerning the target problem.

DOI: 10.4324/9781003508472-12

4. Assess A – establish the inference/s concerning the target problem that is/are triggering irrational beliefs (B).
5. Assess G – establish how and to what extent A impedes G in the target problem. Also, support and encourage eudaimonic goals.
6. Teach the B-C connection – educate the client in the idea of cognitive mediation.
7. Assess B – establish the existence and nature of irrational beliefs (iB) and rational beliefs (rB).
8. Teach the client about iBs and rBs, and how to distinguish between them.
9. Ensure client is able to see the connection between their Gs, As, Bs, and Cs.
10. Disputation (D) – challenge and weaken irrational beliefs.
11. Effective New Belief (E) – develop, challenge, strengthen, and commit to rational beliefs.
12. Ensure redundancy – client becomes their own "practitioner".

When finishing the work with a client we of course need to have ameliorated the issue for which they sought our help. But also, through REBT we should be encouraging the client to become their own therapist (Dryden et al., 2010), in effect making ourselves as practitioners redundant. In REBT we help the client to learn, develop, strengthen, and refine particular ideas and skills that facilitate their progression towards fulfilment. The client has only really learned an idea or skill when they can apply those ideas and skills independently. The client may demonstrate learning in sessions where there is an intense repetition of disputation and rational belief rehearsal. But has the client *retained* this learning to the extent that they can dispute beliefs as they emerge in life, away from the practitioner? The goal should be to ensure the client understands and can apply REBT by themselves, and that emotional insight is either partially achieved or can be worked towards by the client autonomously. The practitioner and client should see emotional insight on the horizon.

For me to be confident that the client can independently apply REBT I need to be able to answer the following questions positively:

1. Does the client understand, and can they accurately articulate each element of, the GABCDE framework?
2. Does the client endorse B-C thinking over A-C thinking?
3. Can the client distinguish between inferential As, and irrational and rational Bs?
4. Does the client understand, and can they demonstrate the application of, the differences between irrational and rational beliefs?
5. Can the client apply disputation rigorously, accurately, and independently?
6. Can the client generate accurate rational beliefs?
7. Does the client have a plan for committing to their new rational beliefs?
8. Does the client understand, and can they recognize in themselves, UNEs and HNEs?
9. Does the client's new behaviour or action tendencies indicate HNEs rather than UNEs?
10. Is the client properly, and rationally, oriented towards their FGs?

I can of course ask the above questions to the client directly, and we can obviously discuss each question, but these questions are more for me and my internal compass, and my answers are based on the client's progress and articulation of REBT in the sessions and in their homework. One effective way for me to able to answer some of these questions is for the client to act as my psychologist and take me through one of my issues. The issue I choose will be something minor and will reflect a fairly innocuous life quibble, but I will try to be as honest as I can with the client in my articulation of my issue. It is the client's job to apply REBT with me as best they can, attempting to cover the main tenets of what they have learned with my issue as a case example. Clearly, I am not expecting advanced level psychology work here, but I am looking for their ability to demonstrate their understanding in line with some of the above questions (not all questions are relevant to this task). If I notice deficits in their understanding, I can discuss this with the client to make sure these deficits are addressed forthrightly.

There is another key criterion by which I base my confidence in the client's readiness to finish the work, and it is this: the client uses meetings to talk generally about their week and the sessions are naturally structureless, unfocussed, and goalless. If this happens, then clearly we have moved past the key issues that were perturbing the client, and therefore, I start to move the client towards considering whether they require ongoing REBT work.

Lastly, I recap everything that we have done in our work together, for the client. I try to provide a brief summary of what was covered and the extent to which we have done what we said we were going to do – in other words, I am verbally reflecting on the extent to which the aims of the work have been met. This is really to make sure that we have been as comprehensive as we can in our work, and to provide an opportunity for the client to flag anything they are still unclear on. It also provides them with some final clarity and motivation to continue to work towards rationality. I would end my work with the client by informing them that I am confident in their capacity to move forward positively, but that support is here if they need it.

Many clients will express apprehension about finishing the work. This is normal, and we must consider the significance of what has taken place in this working alliance. It is likely that the relationship you have developed with the client is unlike any other relationship the client has ever experienced. You as the practitioner have dedicated time, attention, and care to the client and their experiences, while taking an empathetic and supportive stance on what they tell you. This is a rare relationship, and as such, losing this relationship can be concerning for clients. Who will they speak to about all these personal issues now? Who will be there to guide and support them as they pursue this uncertain and dangerous career? This is why it is important that we never fully close the door to clients. It is always possible for the client to reach out with additional issues, or just for a catch up and refresher on their REBT knowledge and skills. But it is vital that we encourage clients to see themselves as competent in REBT, autonomous in their usage of REBT, and as someone who can help others with the newly learned REBT skills. I am also of course borrowing here from the basic psychological needs of self-determination theory (SDT; Deci & Ryan, 2002), but this provides a framework for helping me to end work safely with clients amidst their apprehension. Clients continue their REBT work independently as they go through life, and like all humans, are in a constant state of becoming (to paraphrase Bob Dylan). So in some ways, work never really stops.

Sorry, the Book Has to End at Some point: Closing Remarks

In this book, I have tried to abridge *The Rational Practitioner* and apply concision to that rather large text. The idea was to create a briefer and more accessible book that cuts to the chase, but still includes vital detail. I have put forth how REBT *can be* practiced and I have tried to make clear that while REBT is no panacea, it is remarkably flexible and thus can help us as practitioners to approach a broad range of client issues. By offering the interdependent GABCDE framework, I hope I have been able to demonstrate to the reader that REBT is not insula or niche. I also hope I have helped the reader to see that the underpinnings of REBT can be found in both ancient and modern works of philosophy and science.

I did not invent REBT, nor do I care if REBT "succeeds" or "fails" (whatever that means), so I believe I can be *somewhat* objective when it comes to REBT. Like any approach to psychology, REBT has its limitations. Frankly, some of the *perceived* limitations of REBT are based on a poor understanding of REBT (e.g., that REBT only focusses on beliefs and belief change). Other limitations are grounded in a philosophical debate often between advocates of second and third wave psychotherapies (e.g., Collard, 2019, and see volume 23, issue 2, 2005 in the *Journal of Rational-Emotive & Cognitive-Behavior Therapy*). I do not see REBT as being better or worse than any other CBT approach, and rarely do I position REBT *against* other approaches. Comparisons between approaches are useful, but never for the purposes of finding a "winner". Use what works, not what looks cool or fashionable. If you use REBT and it works, keep using it. If you use it and it does not work, then do something else.

To close out this book, there is just one further issue I want to cover, which concerns what we could call REBT when using it non-clinically, as I do.

Rational Emotive Behavioural *Approach* (REBA)

Big question: Do we really need the "T" in "REBT"? Well, yes and no. I'll cover the "yes" first. In academic literature, I believe it is important to use "REBT" in reporting what we are doing even when we are not working "therapeutically" for example in non-clinical and non-therapeutic settings (e.g., performance coaching, life coaching, sport and performance psychology). The reason for this is threefold. First, when we are using REBT non-therapeutically, we are not changing REBT. We are using the same ideas, principles, and processes as those working therapeutically, and thus, let us just call it what it is. Second, to ensure parity of reporting in academic literature, I believe we should call it "REBT" consistently. This aids reviewers of the prevailing literature and helps the field take more accurate stock of research findings and writing pertaining to REBT. Third, we can better connect the past with the present by using "REBT", because for decades now we have reported "REBT", and so if I suddenly started calling REBT something different, how can we connect current writings with older writings? So, for consistency of academic reporting, I am advocating for the use of "REBT", regardless of the context it is applied in (e.g., business, clinical, sport).

However, outside of academic writing, we can of course call REBT whatever we like. As a practitioner, part of the job is to make REBT appealing to potential clients. Therefore, if I want to label REBT as "Smarter Thinking" as I do in my own practice (Turner, 2014), then I am doing so because it fits my audience. In my experience, the word "therapy" is not helpful in some settings because of its clinical connotations and conflation with the physical domain. Sports therapists are not psychologists in sport; they are closer to physiotherapists than psychotherapists. When working within organizations non-clinically, an important job is to reduce barriers to engaging in psychology, and the word "therapy" can be a barrier.

Perhaps a middle ground is needed that reflects the many ways in which REBT is applied therapeutically and non-therapeutically. I offer the term "Rational Emotive Behavioural Approach (REBA)" as a way to communicate that what we are doing is rational-emotive behavioural in nature, but is not always therapeutic or done in a therapeutic or clinical space. In other words, REBT is not always done in clinical settings with people presenting with clinical issues. Indeed, as the performance and coaching literature grows, much REBT work is outside of the clinical space with individuals without a clinical diagnosis. Therefore, perhaps REBA is a more flexible and accommodating moniker for REBT when applied non-therapeutically, and perhaps sheds some of the clinical connotations that "therapy" seems to provoke. If one is to use REBA in academic writing, one should do so in a way that also references REBT explicitly as the actual intervention. REBA might represent the work we do that does not entirely follow the REBT process I have outlined in this book. For example, if using elements of REBT in an isolated and modular fashion, such as rational self-talk (Turner et al., 2020b), the rational credo (ARRC; Turner, 2016a), rational-emotive personal-disclosure mutual-sharing (REPDMS; Vertopolous & Turner, 2017), or the Smarter Thinking App (Turner & Wood, 2019a), it could be described as being an REBA to the work.

Conclusions

REBT is just one of the many psychotherapeutic approaches one could pursue. I am not an REBT evangelist, and do not believe that REBT is best thing since sliced bread. But practitioners might be wondering why they should bother with REBT, and what REBT could offer their clients. I hope that I have provided a good case for REBT in this book, and I hope the book will prove to be interesting and useful to those who read it. To reiterate, this book was developed as a briefer and snappier sister text to the more expansive and more detail **The Rational Practitioner**. As such, my aim here was not to be comprehensive, but I hope I have included enough detail to enable readers to work REBT into their practice, and hope I have encouraged readers to undertake further REBT reading and training. Lastly, I leave you with a quote from Albert Ellis, which I think communicates nicely some of what REBT has to offer.

> *REBT tries to go beyond the rest of the CBTs by showing its clients and others that they are constructively able, albeit with considerable work and practice, to make a profound cognitive-emotional-behavioral change, so that if they encounter some of the worst adversities in the present or future, they will still only make themselves moderately anxious and regretful instead of panicked and depressed. Then, REBT again hypothesizes, individuals will be better able to change what they can change, to accept (but still dislike) what they cannot change, and . . . to have the wisdom to know the difference.*
>
> -Ellis (2003b, p. 17)

References

Agence France-Presse. (2015, October 26). *It is not the end of the world: Jurgen Klopp after Liverpool's draw*. NDTV Sports. http://sports.ndtv.com/english-premier-league/news/250752-it-is-not-the-end-of-the-world-jurgen-klopp-after-liverpool-s-draw

Alegria, K. E., & Cameron, L. D. (2020). Cognitive mediators. In M. Gellman (Ed.), *Encyclopedia of behavioral medicine* (2nd ed., pp. 496–497). Springer International Publishing.

Andersen, M. B. (2009). The "canon" of psychological skills training for enhancing performance. In K. F. Hays (Ed.), *Performance psychology in action: A casebook for working with athletes, performing artists, business leaders, and professionals in high-risk occupations* (pp. 11–34). American Psychological Association. https://doi.org/10.1037/11876-001

Armstrong, L. M. (2017). Rational emotive therapy. In V. Zeigler-Hill & T. Shackelford (Eds.), *Encyclopedia of personality and individual differences*. Springer. https://doi.org/10.1007/978-3-319-28099-8_996-1

Atkinson, M. (2014, September). *The Psychologist, 27*.

Babić, V., Sarac, J., Missoni, S., & Sindik, J. (2015). Athletic engagement and athletic identity in top croatian sprint runners. *Collegium Antropologicum, 39*(3), 521–528.

Bandura, A. (1997). *Self-efficacy: The exercise of control*. Freeman.

Bandura, A. (2006). Toward a psychology of human agency. *Perspectives on Psychological Science, 1*, 164–180.

Beck, A. T. (1976). *Cognitive therapy and the emotional disorders*. International Universities Press.

Beck, A. T. (2015). Theory of personality disorders. In A. T. Beck, D. D. Davis, & A. Freeman (Eds.), *Cognitive therapy of personality disorders* (3rd ed., pp. 19–62). Guilford Press.

Beck, A. T., & Emery, G. (1985). *Anxiety disorders and phobias: A cognitive perspective*. Basic.

Beck, A. T., & Freeman, A. M. (1990). *Cognitive therapy of personality disorders*. Guilford Press.

Bennett, R., & Oliver, J. E. (2019). *Acceptance and commitment therapy: 100 key points and techniques*. Routledge/Taylor & Francis Group. https://doi.org/10.4324/9781351056144

Bernard, M. E. (1985). A rational-emotive mental training program for professional athletes. In A. Ellis & M. E. Bernard (Eds.), *Clinical applications of rational-emotive therapy* (pp. 227–309). Plenum.

Bernard, M. E. (2009). Dispute irrational beliefs and teach rational beliefs: An interview with Albert Ellis. *Journal of Rational-Emotive & Cognitive-Behavior Therapy, 27*(1), 67–77. https://doi.org/10.1007/s10942-009-0089-x.

Bernard, M. E., & Dryden, W. (2019). *Advances in REBT: Theory, practice, research, measurement, prevention and promotion*. Springer Nature.

Bishop, F. M. (2000). Helping clients manage addictions with REBT. *Journal of Rational-Emotive & Cognitive-Behavior Therapy, 18*, 127–151. https://doi.org/10.1023/A:1007874820119

Bond, J. (2002). Applied sport psychology: Philosophy, reflections, and experience. *International Journal of Sport Psychology, 33*, 19–37.
Bordin, E. S. (1979). The generalizability of the psychoanalytic concept of the working alliance. *Psychotherapy: Theory, Research & Practice, 16*(3), 252–260. https://doi.org/10.1037/h0085885
Bowman, A., & Turner, M. J. (2022). When time is of the essence: The use of Rational Emotive Behavior Therapy (REBT) informed single-session therapy (SST) to alleviate social and golf-specific anxiety, and improve well-being and performance, in amateur golfers. *Psychology of Sport and Exercise*. Accepted February 15, 2022.
Breitmeyer, A. M., & Turner, M. J. (2018). Sport coaching. In M. Bernard & O. David (Eds.), *Coaching for rational living*. Springer.
Brewer, B. W., & Cornelius, A. E. (2001). Norms and factorial invariance of the athletic identity measurement scale. *Academic Athletic Journal, 16*, 103–113.
Brewer, B. W., Van Raalte, J. L., & Linder, D. E. (1991). Construct validity of the athletic identity measurement scale. *Proceedings of the North American Society for the Psychology of Sport and Physical Activity Annual Conference*. Monterey, CA, USA. June 13–16, 1991.
Brewer, B. W., Van Raalte, J. L., & Linder, D. E. (1993). Athletic identity: Hercules' muscles or Achilles heel? *International Journal of Sport Psychology, 24*(2), 237–254.
Browne, C. M., Dowd, E. T., & Freeman, A. (2010). *Rational and irrational beliefs and psychopathology*. In D. David, S. J. Lynn, & A. Ellis (Eds.), *Rational and irrational beliefs: Research, theory, and clinical practice* (pp. 149–171). Oxford University Press.
Cannizzaro, M. (2019, April 7). *How Rory McIlroy is now dealing with career Grand Slam pressure*. New York Post. Retrieved March 17, 2022, from https://nypost.com/2019/04/06/how-rory-mcilroy-is-now-dealing-with-career-grand-slam-pressure/
Carver, C. S., & Scheier, M. F. (1998). *On the self-regulation of behavior*. Cambridge University Press.
Caserta, D. A., Dowd, E. T., Lynn, S. J., David, D., & Ellis, A. (2010). Rational and irrational beliefs in primary prevention and mental health. In D. David, S. J. Lynn, & A. Ellis (Eds.), *The role of rational and irrational beliefs in human functioning and disturbances: Implications for research, theory, and clinical practice*. Oxford University Press.
CCBT. (2021, June 13). *REBT helps you accept reality – Like it or not*. College of Cognitive Behavioural Therapies. Retrieved March 12, 2022, from https://www.cbttherapies.org.uk/2021/06/13/rebt-helps-you-accept-reality-like-it-or-not/
Chadha, N., Turner, M. J., & Slater, M. J. (2019). Investigating irrational beliefs, cognitive appraisals, challenge and threat, and affective states in golfers approaching competitive situations. *Frontiers in Psychology*. https://doi.org/10.3389/fpsyg.2019.02295
Chadha, N. J., Turner, M. J., & Slater, M. J. (2024). Examination of cognitive appraisals, irrational beliefs, and challenge and threat evaluations in the prediction of tournament affective states and performance of competitive elite Indian golfers. *Stress and Health: Journal of the International Society for the Investigation of Stress, 40*(3), e3342. https://doi.org/10.1002/smi.3342
Channel 4 Paralympics [C4 Paralympics]. (2021, August 31). *'The British public have proven to me that you don't need medals to be someone'* [Tweet]. Twitter. https://twitter.com/C4Paralympics/status/1432630042757058563
Chrysidis, S., Turner, M. J., & Wood, A. G. (2020). The effects of REBT on irrational beliefs, self-determined motivation, and self-efficacy in American Football. *Journal of Sports Sciences, 38*(19), 2215–2224. https://doi.org/10.1080/02640414.2020.1776924
Cisler, J. M., & Koster, E. H. (2010). Mechanisms of attentional biases towards threat in anxiety disorders: An integrative review. *Clinical Psychology Review, 30*(2), 203–216. https://doi.org/10.1016/j.cpr.2009.11.003
Clark, D. A. (2014). Cognitive restructuring: A major contribution of cognitive therapy. In: S. G. Hofmann & D. J. A. Dozois (Eds.), *Cognitive behavioral therapy: A complete reference guide, Vol. 1. CBT general techniques* (pp. 23–45). Wiley-Blackwell.
Claspell, E. (2010). Cognitive-behavioral therapies. In S. J. Hanrahan & M. B. Andersen (Eds.), *Routledge handbook of applied sport psychology* (pp. 131–140). Routledge.

Collard, J. J. (2019). ACT vs CBT: An exercise in idiosyncratic language. *International Journal of Cognitive Therapy, 12*(2), 126–145. https://doi.org/10.1007/s41811-019-00043-9
Collard, J. J. (2022). Cognitive-behavioural therapy (CBT). In M. J. Turner, M. V. Jones, & A. W. Wood (Eds.), *Applying cognitive behavioural therapeutic (CBT) approaches in sport*. Routledge.
Costa, S., Santi, G., di Fronso, S., Montesano, C., Di Gruttola, F., Ciofi, E. G., Morgilli, L., & Bertollo, M. (2020). Athletes and adversities: Athletic identity and emotional regulation in time of COVID–19. *Sport Sciences for Health, 16*(4), 609–618. https://doi.org/10.1007/s11332-020-00677-9
Craske, M. G., Treanor, M., Conway, C. C., Zbozinek, T., & Vervliet, B. (2014). Maximizing exposure therapy: An inhibitory learning approach. *Behaviour Research and Therapy, 58*(1), 10–23. https://doi.org/10.1016/j.brat.2014.04.006
Crawford, T., & Ellis, A. (1989). A dictionary of rational-emotive feelings and behaviors. *Journal of Rational-Emotive & Cognitive-Behavior Therapy, 7*(1), 3–28. https://doi.org/10.1007/BF02175569
David, A., Ghinea, C., Macavei, B., & Eva, K. (2005). A search for "hot" cognitions in a clinical and non-clinical context: Appraisal, attributions, core relational themes, irrational beliefs, and their relations to emotion. *Journal of Cognitive-Behavioral Psychotherapy, 5*, 1–42.
David, D. (2015). Rational emotive behavior therapy. In R. L. Cautin & S. O. Lilienfeld (Eds.), *Encyclopedia of clinical psychology*. Wiley-Blackwell.
David, D., Cotet, C., Matu, S., Mogoase, C., & Stefan, S. (2018). 50 years of rational-emotive and cognitive-behavioral therapy: A systematic review and meta-analysis. *Journal of Clinical Psychology, 74*(3), 304–318. https://doi.org/10.1002/jclp.22514
David, D., & Cramer, D. (2010). Rational and irrational beliefs in human feelings and psychophysiology. In D. David, S. J. Lynn, & A. Ellis (Eds.), *Rational and irrational beliefs* (pp. 99–114). Oxford University Press.
David, D., Lynn, S. J., & Ellis, A. (2010). *Rational and irrational beliefs: Research, theory, and clinical practice* (Illustrated ed.). Oxford University Press.
David, D., Miclea, M., & Opre, A. (2004). The information-processing approach to the human mind: Basics and beyond. *Journal of Clinical Psychology, 60*(4), 353–368. https://doi.org/10.1002/jclp.10250
David, D., Schnur, J., & Belloiu. A. (2002). Another search for the "hot" cognitions: Appraisal, irrational beliefs, attributions, and their relation to emotion. *Journal of Rational-Emotive & Cognitive-Behavior Therapy, 20*(2), 93–131.
David, O. A., Cîmpean, A., Costescu, C., DiGiuseppe, R., Doyle, K., Hickey, M., & David, D. (2021). Effectiveness of outpatient rational emotive behavior therapy over one decade. *American Journal of Psychotherapy, 74*(4), 157–164. https://doi.org/10.1176/appi.psychotherapy.20200009
Deci, E. L., & Ryan, R. M. (2002). Self-determination research: Reflections and future directions. In E. L. Deci & R. M. Ryan (Eds.), *Handbook of self-determination research.* University of Rochester Press.
Deen, S., Turner, M. J., & Wong, R. (2017). The effects of REBT and credos on irrational beliefs and resilient qualities in athletes. *The Sport Psychologist, 31*, 249–263.
DiGiuseppe, R. (1986). The implication of the philosophy of science for rational-emotive theory and therapy. *Psychotherapy: Theory, Research, Practice, Training, 23*(4), 634–639. https://doi.org/10.1037/h0085668
DiGiuseppe, R. (1991). Comprehensive cognitive disputing in RET. In M. Bernard (Ed.), *Using rational-emotive therapy effectively: A practitioner's guide*. Plenum.
DiGiuseppe, R., Leaf, R., Exner, T., & Robin, M. V. (1988). *The development of a measure of rational/irrational thinking*. Paper presented at the World Congress of Behavior Therapy, Edinburgh, Scotland.
DiGiuseppe, R. A., Doyle, K. A., Dryden, W., & Backx, W. (2014). *A practitioner's guide to rational emotive behavior therapy* (3rd ed.). Oxford University Press.

DiLorenzo, T. A., David, D., & Montgomery, G. H. (2007). The interrelations between irrational cognitive processes and distress in stressful academic settings. *Personality and Individual Differences, 42*, 765–777.
Dobson, K. S., & Dozois, D. J. A. (2010). Historical and philosophical bases of the cognitive-behavioral therapies. In K. S. Dobson (Ed.), *Handbook of cognitive-behavioral therapies* (3rd ed., pp. 3–38). The Guilford Press.
Dobson, K. S., & Shaw, B. F. (1988). The use of treatment manuals in cognitive therapy: Experience and issues. *Journal of Consulting and Clinical Psychology, 56*, 673–680.
Dryden, W. (1987). *Current issues in rational-emotive therapy*. Croom Helm.
Dryden, W. (1989). The use of chaining in rational-emotive therapy. *Journal of Rational-Emotive & Cognitive-Behavior Therapy, 7*(2), 59–66. https://doi.org/10.1007/BF01246504
Dryden, W. (1994). Reason and emotion in psychotherapy: Thirty years on. *Journal of Rational-Emotive Cognitive-Behavioral Therapy, 12*, 83–99. https://doi.org/10.1007/BF02354606
Dryden, W. (1995). *Preparing for client change in rational emotive behavior therapy*. Whurr.
Dryden, W. (2007). Resilience and rationality. *Journal of Rational-Emotive & Cognitive-Behavior Therapy, 25*(3), 213–226. https://doi.org/10.1007/s10942-006-0050-1
Dryden, W. (2008). *Distinctive features of rational emotive behaviour therapy*. Brunner-Routledge.
Dryden, W. (2009a). *Skills in rational emotive behaviour counselling and psychotherapy*. Sage.
Dryden, W. (2009b). *How to think and intervene like an REBT therapist* (1st ed.). Routledge.
Dryden, W. (2012a). *The ABCs of REBT revisited: Perspectives on conceptualization*. Springer.
Dryden, W. (2012b). The "ABCs" of REBT III: A study of errors and confusions made by Ellis and Joffe Ellis (2011). *Journal of Rational-Emotive and Cognitive-Behavior Therapy, 30*(3), 188–201. https://doi.org/10.1007/s10942–011-0140-6
Dryden, W. (2012c). On rational beliefs in rational emotive behavior therapy: A theoretical perspective. *Journal of Rational-Emotive & Cognitive-Behavior Therapy, 31*(1), 39–48. https://doi.org/10.1007/s10942-012-0158-4
Dryden, W. (2013). *Rationality and pluralism*. Routledge.
Dryden, W. (2016). *When time is at a premium: Cognitive-behavioural approaches to single session therapy and very brief coaching*. Rationality Publications.
Dryden, W. (2017). Rational emotive behaviour therapy. In C. Feltham, T. Hanley, & L. A. Winter (Eds.), *The SAGE handbook of counselling and psychotherapy* (4th ed.). SAGE Publications Ltd.
Dryden, W. (2018). *Very brief therapeutic conversations* (1st ed.). Routledge.
Dryden, W. (2019a). The distinctive features of rational emotive behavior therapy. In: M. Bernard & W. Dryden (Eds.), *Advances in REBT* (pp. 23–46). Springer. https://doi.org/10.1007/978-3-319-93118-0_8
Dryden, W. (2019b). Rational emotive behavior therapy: Assessment, conceptualisation and intervention. In M. Bernard & W. Dryden (Eds.), *Advances in REBT*. Springer. https://doi.org/10.1007/978-3-319-93118-0_8
Dryden, W. (2019c). Rational emotive behaviour therapy and the working alliance. In M. Bernard & W. Dryden (Eds.), *Advances in REBT*. Springer. https://doi.org/10.1007/978-3-319-93118-0_8
Dryden, W. (2021). *Reason to change: A rational emotive behaviour therapy workbook 2nd edition* (2nd ed.). Routledge.
Dryden, W. (2022). *The REBT therapist's pocket companion* (2nd ed.). Albert Ellis Institute.
Dryden, W., & Branch, R. (2008). *The fundamentals of rational emotive behaviour therapy: A training handbook* (2nd ed.). Wiley.
Dryden, W., & David, D. (2008). Rational emotive behavior therapy: Current status. *Journal of Cognitive Psychotherapy, 22*(3), 195–209. https://doi.org/10.1891/0889-8391.22.3.195

Dryden, W., & Neenan, M. (1995). *Dictionary of rational emotive behavior therapy*. Wiley.
Dryden, W., & Neenan, M. (2020). *Rational emotive behaviour therapy: 100 key points and techniques* (3rd ed.). Routledge.
Dryden, W., Beal, D., Jones, J., & Trower, P. (2010). The REBT competency scale for clinical and research applications. *Journal of Rational-Emotive & Cognitive-Behavior Therapy, 28*(4), 165–216. https://doi.org/10.1007/s10942-010-0111-3
Dubois, P. (1905). *The psychic treatment of nervous disorders: The psychoneuroses and their moral treatment* (pp. 367–368). Funk & Wagnalls.
Dubois, P (1906). *The influence of the mind on the body* (L. B. Gallatin, Trans., 5th ed.). Funk & Wagnalls.
Dubois, P. (1909). *Psychic treatment of nervous diseases* (6th ed.). *Funk & Wagnalls Company*.
Edison, B. R., Christino, M. A., & Rizzone, K. H. (2021). Athletic identity in youth athletes: A systematic review of the literature. *International Journal of Environmental Research and Public Health, 18*(14), 7331. https://doi.org/10.3390/ijerph18147331
Ellis, A. (1962). *Reason and emotion in psychotherapy*. Lyle Stuart.
Ellis, A. (1963). Toward a more precise definition of "emotional" and "intellectual" insight. *Psychological Reports, 13*(1), 125–126. https://doi.org/10.2466/pr0.1963.13.1.125
Ellis, A. (1973). *Humanistic psychotherapy: The rational-emotive approach*. McGraw-Hill.
Ellis, A. (1976). The biological basis of human irrationality. *Journal of Individual Psychology, 32*(2), 145–168.
Ellis, A. (1977). Rejoinder: Elegant and inelegant RET. *The Counseling Psychologist, 7*(1), 73–82. https://doi.org/10.1177/001100007700700110
Ellis, A. (1979). Is rational-emotive therapy stoical, humanistic, or spiritual? *Journal of Humanistic Psychology, 19*(3), 89–92. https://doi.org/10.1177/002216787901900314
Ellis, A. (1980). Rational-emotive therapy and cognitive behavior therapy: Similarities and differences. *Cognitive Therapy and Research, 4*(4), 325–340.
Ellis, A. (1983). *The case against religiosity*. Institute for Rational Emotive Therapy.
Ellis, A. (1987a). Yes, how reasonable is rational-emotive therapy? *Review of Existential Psychology and Psychiatry, 19*, 135–139
Ellis, A. (1987b). On the origin and development of rational-emotive theory. In W. Dryden (Ed.), *Key cases in psychotherapy* (pp. 148–175). New York University Press.
Ellis, A. (1988). *How to stubbornly refuse to make yourself miserable: About anything – Yes, anything!* (p. 11). Little, Brown Book Group. Kindle Edition.
Ellis, A. (1991). Achieving self-actualization: The rational-emotive approach. *Journal of Social Behavior & Personality, 6*(5), 1–18.
Ellis, A. (1994). *Reason and emotion in psychotherapy* (2nd ed.). Carol Publishing Group.
Ellis, A. (1995). Changing rational emotive therapy (RET) to rational emotive behaviour therapy (REBT). *Journal of Rational-Emotive and Cognitive-Behavior Therapy, 13*(3), 85–89.
Ellis, A. (1996a). *How to stubbornly refuse to make yourself miserable about anything – Yes, anything*. Lyle Stuart Inc.
Ellis, A. (1996b). The humanism of rational emotive behavior therapy and other cognitive behavior therapies. *The Journal of Humanistic Education and Development, 35*(2), 69–88. https://doi.org/10.1002/j.2164-4683.1996.tb00356.x
Ellis, A. (1996c). *REBT diminishes much of the human ego* (Rev. ed.). Albert Ellis Institute.
Ellis, A. (2001). *Feeling better, getting better, staying better: Profound self-help therapy for your emotions*. Impact.
Ellis, A. (2002a). *Overcoming resistance: A rational emotive behavior therapy integrated approach* (2nd ed.). Springer Publishing Co.
Ellis, A. (2002b). The role of irrational beliefs in perfectionism. In G. L. Flett & P. L. Hewitt (Eds.), *Perfectionism: Theory, research, and treatment* (pp. 217–229). American Psychological Association. https://doi.org/10.1037/10458-009

Ellis, A. (2003a). Early theories and practices of rational emotive behavior therapy and how they have been augmented and revised during the last three decades. *Journal of Rational-Emotive & Cognitive-Behavior Therapy, 21*(3/4), 219–243.

Ellis, A. (2003b). The relationship of rational emotive behavior therapy (REBT) to social psychology. *Journal of Rational-Emotive & Cognitive-Behavior Therapy, 21*(1), 5–20. https://doi.org/10.1023/A:1024177000887

Ellis, A. (2004). *The road to tolerance: The philosophy of rational emotive behaviour therapy*. Prometheus.

Ellis, A. (2005a). Can rational-emotive behavior therapy (REBT) and acceptance and commitment therapy (ACT) resolve their differences and be integrated? *Journal of Rational-Emotive & Cognitive-Behavior Therapy, 23*(2), 153–168. https://doi.org/10.1007/s10942-005-0008-8

Ellis, A. (2005b). *The myth of self-esteem: How rational emotive behavior therapy can change your life forever (psychology)*. Prometheus.

Ellis, A., David, D., & Lynn, S. J. (2010). Rational and irrational beliefs: A historical and conceptual perspective. In D. David, S. J. Lynn, & A. Ellis (Eds.), *Rational and irrational beliefs: Research, theory, and clinical practice* (pp. 3–22). Oxford University Press.

Ellis, A., & DiGiuseppe, R. (1993). Are inappropriate or dysfunctional feelings in rational-emotive therapy qualitative or quantitative? *Cognitive Therapy and Research, 5*, 471–477.

Ellis, A., & Dryden, W. (1997). *The practice of rational emotive behavior therapy* (2nd ed.). Springer Publishing Co.

Ellis, A., & Harper, R. A. (1975). *A new guide to rational living*. Prentice-Hall.

Ellis, A., & MacLaren, C. (1998). *Rational emotive behavior therapy: A therapist's guide*. Impact Publishers.

Elvins, M., Miller, A., & Turner, M. J. (2025). Examining the effects rational emotive behaviour therapy (REBT) with embedded athlete rational resilience credo (ARRC) on the irrational beliefs, motivation regulation, and mental health of student-athletes. *Journal of Rational-Emotive & Cognitive-Behavior Therapy, 43*. https://doi.org/10.1007/s10942-025-00619-9

Engels, G. I., Garnefski, N., & Diekstra, R. F. (1993). Efficacy of rational-emotive therapy: A quantitative analysis. *Journal of Consulting and Clinical Psychology, 61*(6), 1083–1090.

Festinger, L. (1957). *A theory of cognitive dissonance*. Stanford University Press.

Festinger, L. (1962, October). Cognitive dissonance. *Scientific American, 207*(4), 93–106.

Finley, R. D. (1979). The spiritual poverty of rational-emotive therapy. *Journal of Humanistic Psychology, 19*(3), 83–87.

Fisher, B. (2020, September 11). *Ben Foster: 'I want to be a cyclist after football. The Alps, Vuelta, Giro'*. Watford | The Guardian. Retrieved March 12, 2022, from https://amp.theguardian.com/football/2020/sep/10/ben-foster-watford-cyclist-after-football-the-alps-vuelta-giro?__twitter_impression=true

Frijda, N. (1986). *The emotions*. Cambridge University Press.

Frijda, N. (1988). The laws of emotion. *American Psychologist, 43*, 349–358.

Gellatly, R., & Beck, A. T. (2016). Catastrophic thinking: A transdiagnostic process across psychiatric disorders. *Cognitive Therapy and Research, 40*(4), 441–452. https://doi.org/10.1007/s10608-016-9763-3

Gonzalez, J. E., Nelson, J. R., Gutkin, T. B., Saunders, A., Galloway, A., & Shwery, C. S. (2004). Rational emotive therapy with children and adolescents a meta-analysis. *Journal of Emotional and Behavioral Disorders, 12*(4), 222–235.

Gross, J. J. (1998). The emerging field of emotion regulation: An integrative review. *Review of General Psychology, 2*(3), 271–299. https://doi.org/10.1037/1089-2680.2.3.271

Hayes, S. C., Levin, M. E., Plumb-Vilardaga, J., Villatte, J. L., & Pistorello, J. (2013). Acceptance and commitment therapy and contextual behavioral science: Examining the progress of a distinctive model of behavioral and cognitive therapy. *Behavior Therapy, 44*(2), 180–198. https://doi.org/10.1016/j.beth.2009.08.002

Hickey, M., & Doyle, K. A. (2018). Rational emotive behavior therapy. In A. Vernon & K. A. Doyle (Eds.), *Cognitive behavior therapies: A guidebook for practitioners* (pp. 109–142). American Counseling Association.

Hofmann, S. G., Asmundson, G. J., & Beck, A. T. (2013). The science of cognitive therapy. *Behavior Therapy*, *44*(2), 199–212. https://doi.org/10.1016/j.beth.2009.01.007

Hofmann, S. G., Sawyer, A. T., & Fang, A. (2010). The empirical status of the 'new wave' of cognitive behavioral therapy. *Psychiatric Clinics of North America*, *33*(3), 701–710. https://doi.org/10.1016/j.psc.2010.04.006.

Horvath, A. O., & Greenberg, L. S. (1989). Development and validation of the working alliance inventory. *Journal of Counseling Psychology*, *36*, 223–233. https://doi.org/10.1037/0022-0167.36.2.223.

Hymen, S. P., & Warren, R. (1978). An evaluation of rational-emotive imagery as a component of rational-emotive therapy in the treatment of test anxiety. *Perceptual and Motor Skills*, *46*(3), 847–853. https://doi.org/10.2466/pms.1978.46.3.847

Jackson, K. (2019, March 27). *Rory McIlroy will not be defined by wins and lossesahead of WGC-Match Play*. Sky Sports. Retrieved March 17, 2022, from https://www.skysports.com/golf/news/12176/11676065/rory-mcilroy-will-not-be-defined-by-wins-and-losses-ahead-of-wgc-match-play

Jones, B. R. (2019, April 8). *Rory: Id love to win Masters but I dont need to any more*. Belfast Telegraph. Retrieved March 17, 2022, from https://www.belfasttelegraph.co.uk/sport/golf/masters/rory-id-love-to-win-masters-but-i-dont-need-to-any-more-37991659.html

Jordana, A., Turner, M. J., Ramis, Y., & Torregrossa, M. (2023). Systematic mapping review on the use of Rational Emotive Behavior Therapy (REBT) with athletes. *International Review of Sport and Exercise* Psychology, *16*(1), 231–256. https://doi.org/10.1080/1750984X.2020.1836673

Kashdan, T., & Biswas-Diener, R. (2014). *The power of negative emotion: How anger, guilt, and self doubt are essential to success and fulfillment*. Oneworld Publications.

Kazantzis, N., Whittington, C., & Datillio, F. (2010). Meta-analysis of homework effects in cognitive and behavioral therapy: A replication and extension. *Clinical Psychology: Science and Practice*, *17*(2), 144–156.

King, A., Plateau, C., Turner, M. J., Young, P., & Barker, J. B. (2024). A systematic review of the nature and efficacy of rational emotive behaviour therapy interventions. *PloS ONE*, *19*(7), e0306835. https://doi.org/10.1371/journal.pone.0306835

Kinney, A. (2000). The intellectual-insight problem: Implications for assessment and rational-emotive behavior therapy. *Journal of Contemporary Psychotherapy*, *30*, 261–272. https://doi.org/10.1023/A:1004142732449

Kreibig, S. D., Gendolla, G. H., & Scherer, K. R. (2010). Psychophysiological effects of emotional responding to goal attainment. *Biological psychology*, *84*(3), 474–487. https://doi.org/10.1016/j.biopsycho.2009.11.004

Kuyken, W., Padesky, C. A., & Dudley, R. (2009). *Collaborative case conceptualization: Working effectively with clients in cognitive-behavioral therapy*. Guilford Press.

Late Show [CBS]. (2017, June 5). *Dave Chappelle Interview on David Letterman (2014)* [Video]. YouTube. https://www.youtube.com/watch?v=kXv39gQ_YEg

Lazarus, A. A. (1995). REBT: A sign of evolution or devolution? An historical perspective. *Journal of Rational-Emotive & Cognitive-Behavior Therapy*, *13*(2), 97–100. https://doi.org/10.1007/bf02354455

Lazarus, R., & Folkman, S. (1984). *Stress, appraisal, and coping*. Springer.

Lazarus, R. S. (1991). *Emotion and adaptation*. Oxford University Press.

Lazarus, R. S. (1999). *Stress and emotion: A new synthesis*. Springer Publishing Co.

Lyons, L. C., & Woods, P. J. (1991). The efficacy of rational-emotive therapy: A quantitative review of the outcome research. *Clinical Psychology Review*, *11*(4), 357–369.

MacInnes, D. (2004). The theories underpinning rational emotive behaviour therapy. *International Journal of Nursing Studies*, *41*, 685–695.

Mahoney, M. J. (1974). *Cognition and behavior modification* (1st ed.). Ballinger Pub. Co.

Mathews, A., & MacLeod, C. (2002). Induced processing biases have causal effects on anxiety. *Cognition and Emotion, 16*(3), 331–354.
Maultsby, M., Jr. (1971). Rational emotive imagery. *Rational Living, 6*(1), 24–27.
Maultsby, M. C. (1975). *Help yourself to happiness trough rational self-counseling.* Institute for Rational Living.
Maultsby, M. C., Jr. (1984). *Rational behavior therapy.* Prentice Hall.
Memon, Z. A., & Treur, J. (2010). On the reciprocal interaction between believing and feeling: An adaptive agent modelling perspective. *Cognitive Neurodynamics, 4*(4), 377–394.
Michel-Kröhler, A., & Turner, M. J. (2022). Link between irrational beliefs and important markers of mental health in a German sample of athletes: Differences between gender, sport-type, and performance level. *Frontiers in Psychology, 13*, 918329. https://doi.org/10.3389/fpsyg.2022.918329
Mobini, S., & Grant, A. (2007). Clinical implications of attentional bias in anxiety disorders: An integrative literature review. *Psychotherapy: Theory, Research, Practice, Training, 44*(4), 450–462.
Moore, R. H. (1983). Inference as '/~ in RET. *British Journal of Cognitive Psychotherapy, 1*(2), 17–23.
Munnick, J., Turner, M. J., & van Niekerkc, L. (2023). Recommendations for integrating psychological skills training (PST) into rational emotive behavioral therapy (REBT). *Journal of Sport Psychology in Action, 15*(4), 235–246. https://doi.org/10.1080/21520704.2023.2245359
Neenan, M., & Dryden, W. (1996). The intricacies of inference chaining. *Journal of Rational-Emotive and Cognitive-Behavior Therapy, 14*(4), 231–243.
Neenan, M., & Dryden, W. (1999a). When laddering and the downward arrow can be used as adjuncts to inference chaining in rebt assessment. *Journal of Rational-Emotive & Cognitive-Behavior Therapy, 17*, 95–104. https://doi.org/10.1023/A:1023000914421
Neenan, M., & Dryden, W. (1999b). *Rational emotive behaviour therapy: Advances in theory and practice*. Whurr.
Neenan, M., & Dryden, W. (2010). *Rational emotive behaviour therapy in a nutshell.* SAGE Publications.
Neenan, M., & Dryden, W. (2015). *Cognitive behaviour therapy: 100 key points and techniques* (2nd ed.). Routledge/Taylor & Francis Group.
Nelson-Jones, R. (2006). *Theory and practice of counselling and therapy* (4th ed.). Sage Publications Ltd.
Oltean, H. R., & David, D. O. (2018). A meta-analysis of the relationship between rational beliefs and psychological distress. *Journal of Clinical Psychology, 74*(6), 883–895. https://doi.org/10.1002/jclp.22562
Pekrun, R. (2006). The control-value theory of achievement emotions: Assumptions, corollaries, and implications for educational research and practice. *Educational Psychology Review, 18*, 315–341.
Pennebaker, J. W. (1989). Confession, inhibition, and disease. In L. Berkowitz (Ed.), *Advances in experimental social psychology* (Vol. 22, pp. 211–244). Academic Press. https://doi.org/10.1016/S0065-2601(08)60309-3
Pennebaker, J. W., & Susman, J. R. (1988). Disclosure of traumas and psychosomatic processes. *Social Science & Medicine, 26*(3), 327–332. https://doi.org/10.1016/0277-9536(88)90397-8
Peterson, J. B. (2017, May 20). *Biblical Series I: Introduction to the Idea of God* [Video]. YouTube. https://www.youtube.com/watch?v=f-wWBGo6a2w&feature=youtu.be
Petitpas, A. (1978). Identity foreclosure: A unique challenge. *Personnel & Guidance Journal, 56*(9).
Pinker, S. (2021). *Rationality: What it is. Why it seems scarce. Why it matters*. Viking.
Priyadarshini, S. D., & Jose, T. P. (2025). Publication trends in rational emotive behavior therapy: A bibliometric analysis of the past three decades. *Current Psychology, 44*(18), 15200–15214. https://doi.org/10.1007/s12144-025-08267-z

Rassin, E., Merckelbach, H., & Muris, P. (2000). Paradoxical and less paradoxical effects of thought suppression: A critical review. *Clinical Psychology Review*, *20*(8), 973–995. https://doi.org/10.1016/s0272-7358(99)00019-7

Raue, P. J., & Goldfried, M. R. (1994). Therapeutic alliance in cognitive-behavior therapy. In A. O. Horvath & L. S. Greenberg (Eds.), *The working alliance: Theory, research and practice* (pp. 131–152). Wiley.

Robb, H. (2003). REBT: Thinking it through once more. In W. Dryden (Ed.), *Rational emotive behaviour therapy: Theoretical developments* (pp. 35–54). Routledge.

Robb, H., Backx, W., & Thomas, J. (1999). The use of cognitive, emotive and behavioral interventions in rational emotive behavior therapy when clients lack "emotional" insight. *Journal of Rational-Emotive & Cognitive Behavior Therapy*, *17*(3), 201–209.

Robb, H., & Ciarrochi, J. (2005). Some final, gulp, "words" on REBT, ACT & RFT. *Journal of Rational-Emotive & Cognitive-Behavior Therapy*, *23*(2), 169–173. https://doi.org/10.1007/s10942-005-0009-7

Robertson, D. (2019). *The philosophy of cognitive-behavioural therapy (cbt): Stoic philosophy as rational and cognitive psychotherapy* (2nd ed.). Routledge.

Robertson, D., & Codd, R. T. (2019). Stoic philosophy as a cognitive-behavioral therapy. *The Behavior Therpist*, *42*(2), 33–60.

Roemer, L., & Borkovec, T. D. (1994). Effects of suppressing thoughts about emotional material. *Journal of Abnormal Psychology*, *103*(3), 467–474. https://doi.org/10.1037//0021-843x.103.3.467

Ruggiero, G. M., Spada, M. M., & Caselli, G. (2018). A historical and theoretical review of cognitive behavioral therapies: from structural self-knowledge to functional processes. *Journal of Rational-Emotive Cognitive-Behavioral Therapy*, *36*(4), 378–403. https://doi.org/10.1007/s10942-018-0292-8

Ruth, W. J. (1992). Irrational thinking in humans: An evolutionary proposal for Ellis' genetic postulate. *Journal of Rational-Emotive & Cognitive-Behavior Therapy*, *10*(1), 3–20. https://doi.org/10.1007/BF01245738

Sarracino, D., Dimaggio, G., Ibrahim, R., Popolo, R., Sassaroli, S., & Ruggiero, G. M. (2017). When REBT goes difficult: Applying ABC-DEF to personality disorders. *Journal of Rational Emotive and Cognitive Behavior Therapy*, *35*, 278–295. https://doi.org/10.1007/s10942-016-0258-7

Seneca. (2010). *On anger* (R. A. Kaster & M. C. Nussbaum, Trans.). University of Chicago Press. (Original work written c. AD 41–52)

Sharf, R. S. (1996). *Theories of psychotherapy and counseling: Concepts and cases*. Brooks/Cole Publishing Company.

Shea, D. (2016). Basic tenets of rebt/cbt. In *Cognitive behavioral approaches for counsellors* (pp. 21–38). SAGE Publications, Inc. https://doi.org/10.4135/9781483393650.n5

Smith, C. A., & Lazarus, R. S. (1993). Appraisal components, core relational themes, and the emotions. *Cognition and Emotion*, *7*(3–4), 233–269. https://doi.org/10.1080/02699939308409189

Sparkes, A. C. (1998). Athletic identity: An Achilles' heel to the survival of self. *Qualitative Health Research*, *8*(5), 644–664.

Spence, S. H., March, S., & Donovan, C. L. (2019). New technologies to deliver CBT: Computer and web-based programs, mobile applications, and virtual reality. In L. J. Farrell, T. H. Ollendick, & P. Muris (Eds.), *Innovations in CBT for childhood anxiety, OCD, and PTSD: Improving access and outcomes* (pp. 73–105). Cambridge University Press. https://doi.org/10.1017/9781108235655.005

Sprenkle, D. H., & Blow, A. J. (2004). Common factors and our sacred models. Journal of Marital and Family Therapy, 30(2), 113–129. https://doi.org/10.1111/j.1752-0606.2004.tb01228.x

Stanovich, K. E., Toplak, M. E., & West, R. F. (2008). The development of rational thought: A taxonomy of heuristics and biases. *Advances in Child Development and Behaviour, 36*, 251–285. https://doi.org/10.1016/s0065-2407(08)00006-2

Stanovich, K. E. (2012). On the distinction between rationality and intelligence: Implications for understanding individual differences in reasoning. In K. Holyoak & R. Morrison (Eds.), *The Oxford handbook of thinking and reasoning* (pp. 343–365). Oxford University Press.

Still, A. (2010). Rationality and rational psychotherapy: The heart of REBT. In D. David, S. J. Lynn, & A. Ellis (Eds.), *Rational and irrational beliefs: Research, theory, and clinical practice* (pp. 23–48). Oxford University Press.

Szentagotai, A., & Jones, J. (2010). The behavioral consequences of irrational beliefs. In D. David, S. J. Lynn, & A. Ellis (Eds.), *Rational and irrational beliefs in human functioning and disturbances*. Oxford University Press.

Taleb, N. N. (2012). *Antifragile: Things that gain from disorder*. Random House.

Trip, S., Vernon, A., & McMahon, J. (2007). Effectiveness of rational-emotive education: A quantitative meta-analytical study. *Journal of Cognitive and Behavioral Psychotherapies, 7*(1), 81–93.

Trower, P., & Jones, J. (2001). How REBT can be less disturbing and remarkably more influential in Britain: A review of views of practitioners and researchers. *Journal of Rational-Emotive & Cognitive-Behavior Therapy, 19*, 21–30. https://doi.org/10.1023/A:1007891115800

Turner, M. J. (2014). Smarter thinking in sport. *The Psychologist, 27*(8), 596–599.

Turner, M. J. (2016a). Proposing a rational resilience credo for athletes. *Journal of Sport Psychology in Action, 7*(3), 170–181. https://doi.org/10.1080/21520704.2016.1236051

Turner, M. J. (2016b). Rational emotive behavior therapy (REBT), irrational and rational beliefs, and the mental health of athletes. *Frontiers: Movement Science and Sport Psychology*. https://doi.org/10.3389/fpsyg.2016.01423

Turner, M. J. (2016c, February 6). *Human>Performer*. The Smarter Thinking Project. Retrieved March 20, 2022, from https://thesmarterthinkingproject.com/humanperformer/

Turner, M. J. (2020b, August 6). *The Olympic games: The rational pursuit of excellence*. MMU News. Retrieved March 1, 2022, from https://www.mmu.ac.uk/hpsc/news-and-media/news/story/?id=12703

Turner, M. J. (2022). *The rational practitioner: The sport and performance psychologist's guide to practicing rational emotive behaviour therapy*. Routledge.

Turner, M. J., Allen, M., Slater, M. J., Barker, J. B., Woodcock, C., Harwood, C. G., & McFadyen, K. (2018b). The development and initial validation of the irrational performance beliefs inventory (iPBI). *European Journal of Psychological Assessment, 34*, 174–180.

Turner, M. J., Aspin, G., Didymus, F., Mack, R., Olusoga, P., Wood, A. G., & Bennett, R. (2020a). One case, five approaches: The application of psychotherapeutic approaches in sport psychology. *The Sport Psychologist, 34*(1), 71–83. https://doi.org/10.1123/tsp.2019-0079

Turner, M. J., & Barker, J. B. (2014). Using rational emotive behavior therapy with athletes. *The Sport Psychologist, 28*(1), 75–90.

Turner, M. J., Carrington, S., & Miller, A. (2019b). Psychological distress across sport participation groups: The mediating effects of secondary irrational beliefs on the relationship between primary irrational beliefs and symptoms of anxiety, anger, and depression. *Journal of Clinical Sport Psychology, 13*(1), 17–40.

Turner, M. J., & Davis, H. (2019). Exploring the effects of rational emotive behaviour therapy (REBT) on the irrational beliefs and self-determined motivation of triathletes. *Journal of Applied Sport Psychology, 31*(3), 253–272. https://doi.org/10.1080/10413200.2018.1446472

Turner, M. J., Chadha, N, J., Davis, H., Deen, M. S., Gilmore, H., Jones, J. K., Goldman, S., & Terjesen, M. (2022a). At the coalface: Practitioner perspectives on applying rational emotive behaviour therapy (REBT) in high performance sport. *Journal of Rational-Emotive & Cognitive-Behavior Therapy*. Accepted May 2, 2022.

Turner, M. J., Evans, A., Fortune, G., & Chadha, N. (2024). "I must make the grade!": The role of cognitive appraisals, irrational beliefs, exam anxiety, and affect, in the academic self-concept of undergraduate students. *Anxiety, Stress, & Coping*, *37*(6), 721–744.

Turner, M. J., Ewen, D., & Barker, J. B. (2020a). An idiographic single-case study examining the use of rational emotive behavior therapy (REBT) with three amateur golfers to alleviate sport performance phobias. *Journal of Applied Sport Psychology*, *32*(2), 186–204.

Turner, M. J., Jones, J., & Wood, A. G. (2018a). Applying the REBT cognitive disputation technique to the binary theory of emotional distress. *Effective Scientist-Practitioner*, *1*(1), 46–64.

Turner, M. J., Kirkham, L., & Wood, A. G. (2019c). Teeing up for success: The effects of rational and irrational self-talk on the putting performance of amateur golfers. *Psychology of Sport & Exercise*, *38*, 148–153. https://doi.org/10.1016/j.psychsport.2018.06.012

Turner, M. J., Simonovic, B., Sheffield, D., Michel-Kroehler, A., Dwyer, R., Carrington, S., Chadha, N., McArthur, J., Outar, L., Wood, A., Stupple, E., & Correa Vione, K. (2026). *A new gold standard for measurement in rational emotive behaviour therapy (REBT)?* The Rational and Irrational Ideas Inventory.

Turner, M. J., & Wood, A. G. (2019a). *The smarter thinking app* (Version 1.0.2). [Mobile app]. Google Play Store. https://play.google.com/store/apps/details?id=com.smarterthinkingprofile.smarterthinking&gl=GB

Turner, M. J., & Wood, A. G. (2019b, August 12). *Smarter thinking | Achieve more by stressing less | FREE profile report*. Smarter Thinking. Retrieved March 9, 2022, from https://smarterthinkingprofile.com/

Turner, M. J., Wood, A. G., Barker, J. B., & Chadha, N. (2020b). Rational self-talk: A rational emotive behaviour therapy (REBT) perspective. In A. T. Latinjak & A. Hatzigeorgiadis (Eds.), *Self-talk in sport* (pp. 109–122). Routledge.

Turner, M. J., Wood, A. G., & Jones, J. J. (2019a). A response to Philip Hyland, Demetris Katsikis, and Chrysoula Kostogiannis on the debate point concerning the binary theory of emotional distress. *Effective Scientist-Practitioner*, 2.

Vertopolous, V., & Turner, M. J. (2017). Examining the effectiveness of a rational emotive personal-disclosure mutual-sharing (REPDMS) intervention on the irrational beliefs, rational beliefs, and emotions of Greek adolescent athletes. *The Sport Psychologist*, *31*, 264–274.

Wallace, S. (2018, July 2). *How Gareth Southgate is using his own bitter failure to end England's penalty curse*. The Telegraph. Retrieved March 12, 2022, from https://www.telegraph.co.uk/world-cup/2018/07/02/gareth-southgate-using-bitter-failure-end-englands-penalty-curse/

Waltman, S. H., & Palermo, A. (2019). Theoretical overlap and distinction between rational emotive behaviour therapy's awfulizing and cognitive therapy's catastrophizing. *Mental Health Review Journal*, *24*(1), 44–50. https://doi.org/10.1108/MHRJ-07-2018-0022

Watson, J., Hilliard, R., & Way, W. (2018). *Counseling and communication skills in sport and performance psychology*. Oxford Research Encyclopedia of Psychology. https://doi.org/10.1093/acrefore/9780190236 557.013.140

Webb, T. L., & Sheeran, P. (2007). How do implementation intentions promote goal attainment? A test of component processes. *Journal of Experimental Social Psychology*, *43*(2), 295–302. https://doi.org/10.1016/j.jesp.2006.02.001

Wegner, D. M., Schneider, D. J., Carter, S. R., & White, T. L. (1987). Paradoxical effects of thought suppression. *Journal of Personality and Social Psychology*, *53*(1), 5–13. https://doi.org/10.1037/0022-3514.53.1.5

Wenzel, A. (2006). Attentional disruption in the presence of negative automatic thoughts. *Behavioral and Cognitive Psychotherapy*, *34*, 385–395.

Wessler, R., & Wessler, R. (1980). *The principles and practice of rational-emotive therapy.* Jossey-Bass.

Wilson, D. S. (2010). Rational and irrational beliefs from an evolutionary perspective. In D. David, S. J. Lynn, & A. Ellis (Eds.), *Rational and irrational beliefs: Research, theory, and clinical practice* (pp. 63–72). Oxford University Press.

Wirga, M., DeBernardi, M., Wirga, A., Wirga, M. L., Banout, M., & Fuller, O. G. (2020). Maultsby's rational behavior therapy: Background, description, practical applications, and recent developments. *Journal of Rational-Emotive & Cognitive-Behavior Therapy, 38*(3), 399–423. https://doi.org/10.1007/s10942-020-00341-8

Wood, A., Mack, R., & Turner, M. J. (2020). Developing self-determined motivation and performance with an elite athlete using motivational interviewing in adjunct to rational emotive behaviour therapy. *Journal of Rational-Emotive & Cognitive-Behavior Therapy, 38*, 540–567.

Woody, S. R., & Adessky, R. S. (2002). Therapeutic alliance, group cohesion, and homework compliance during cognitive-behavioral group treatment of social phobia. *Behavior Therapy, 33*, 5–27.

Ziegler, D. J. (2003). The concept of psychological health in rational emotive behavior therapy. *Journal of Rational-Emotive & Cognitive-Behavior Therapy, 21*, 21–36. https://doi.org/10.1023/A:1024129117726

Zupan, B., & Eskritt, M. (2020). Eliciting emotion ratings for a set of film clips: A preliminary archive for research in emotion. *The Journal of Social Psychology, 160*(6), 768–789.

Index

Note: Page references in *italics* indicate figures.

adversity or activating event (A): assume A is true, principle 48; categories 46; critical A 46–8; emotions 45; idiosyncratic 45
anti-awfulizing 67
Athlete Rational Resilience Credo (ARRC) 98
awfulizing 65–7

Beck, A. T. 73
beliefs: athletic identity 71, 72; awfulizing *vs.* anti-awfulizing 65–8; beliefs 58–9, 74; choice 78; critical and analytical approach 82; criticism 72; demandingness *vs.* preferences 60–3; depreciation (global evaluation) *vs.* unconditional acceptance 68–9; FI *vs.* FT 63–5; Dubois method 78–9; GABCDE framework 75; human-worth 69–71; hypotheses 76–8; irrational 75, 80, 81; practitioners 73; rational and irrational beliefs 59–60; REBT, rationality 57; triggering 79–80
Biswas-Diener, R. 34

choice-based assessment of IBs 78
cognitive appraisal theory (CAT) 14
cognitive behavioural therapies (CBTs) 5
consecutive (IB then RB) disputation 87
consequences: assessing C 41–2; emotion flavour 42–3; healthy versus unhealthy negative emotions 34–40; HNE example 43; UNE example 43–4

deductive hypotheses driven assessment 76, 77
demandingness 6, 62
depreciation beliefs 68
DiGiuseppe, R. 26, 68, 76, 77, 92
disputation, assessing: arguments 87–90; client learning 85; collaborative (client-practitioner) argument 83; GABC elements 84; HNE 87; modification-elimination difficulty 84; paired components rating 92; scientists in cahoots 86; socratic comparison 91–2; styles 92–3; UNE 87
Dryden, W. 10, 15, 18, 20, 26, 47, 49, 61, 91, 93, 98
Dryden's choice-based approach 78
Dubois method 78–9

effective new beliefs (E): anti-awfulizing 94; rational self-talk 99–101; imagery 101–102; debate and role play 103; emotional insight 103; intellectual insight 104; caring less 104; HNEs 105; "if-then plans" 102–3; developing rational beliefs 94–6; emotional insight 96–7; promoting and reinforcing rational beliefs 97–8; rational Credo 98–9
Ellis, A. 5, 8, 9, 13, 17, 20, 47, 50, 51, 53, 56, 62, 69, 72, 75, 79, 84, 95, 100, 104, 111

flooding 100
foundational factors, REBT: client 24; homework 27–30; practitioner 23–4; REBT process 26–7; typical programme 32–3; typical session 30–2; work aim 25–6; working alliance 25
frustration intolerance (FI) 60, 63
frustration tolerance (FT) 6, 60, 63

GABCDE framework: adversity (A) 10; beliefs (rational or irrational) (B) 11; CAT 14, *16*, 21; complications 20–1; consequences (C) 11; disputation (D) 11; effective new beliefs (E) 12; emotion regulation theory 9; goals(G) 10; interdependent 17, *19*; intimate interconnections 17–8; irrational beliefs 15; practical opportunities 19–20; rational *vs.* irrational 12; reciprocity 18–19; specific *vs.* general REBT 22; stoicism 13
global evaluation (GE) 60
goals, REBT: career-shortening injury 52; clients 52, 56; critical A 51; FGs 50, 53–5; HNEs or UNEs 51, 52; PGs 50, 53–5; practitioners 53, 54; rational goal pursuit 55

Health Care Professions Council (HCPC) 3

if-then plans 102
irrational beliefs (iBs) 7, 53; *see also* beliefs

Lazarus, R. S. 14, 43, 50, 101
light bulb moment 76

Neenan, M. 49, 91

rational beliefs (rBs) 7
Rational Credo 98
rational emotive behaviour therapy (REBT): BTED 7; CBT 5, 6, 109; client 107, 108; dysfunctional/maladaptive emotions 2; GABCDE framework *7*, 109; human beings 3; practitioner 1; psycho-educational framework4; specific/preferential/elegant 5; therapy 3; UNEs 8
rational emotive behavioural approach (REBA) 109–10
rationality: athletic identity 71, 72; awfulizing *vs.* anti-awfulizing 65–8; beliefs 58–9, 74; criticism 72; demandingness *vs.* preferences 60–3; depreciation (global evaluation) *vs.* unconditional acceptance 68–9; FI *vs.* FT 63–5; human-worth 69–71; practitioners 73; rational and irrational beliefs 59–60; REBT 57
rational kit of cognitive tools 58
The Rational Practitioner (Turner) 1, 19, 109, 110
REBT-I Model 6

Stanovich, K. 57

Turner, M. J. 8, 35, 58, 98; *The Rational Practitioner* 1, 19, 109, 110

unconditional self/other/world acceptance (USA/UOA/UWA) 6
unhealthy negative emotions (UNE) 7, 97

For Product Safety Concerns and Information please contact our EU representative GPSR@taylorandfrancis.com Taylor & Francis Verlag GmbH, Kaufingerstraße 24, 80331 München, Germany

Batch number: 10783740

Printed by Printforce, the Netherlands